Travel and Tourism Public Relations

Travel and Tourism Public Relations

An Introductory Guide for Hospitality Managers

DENNIS E. DEUSCHL, APR

Adjunct Professor, Public Relations Certificate Program
University of Virginia

ELSEVIER
BUTTERWORTH
HEINEMANN

AMSTERDAM • BOSTON • HEIDELBERG • LONDON
NEW YORK • OXFORD • PARIS • SAN DIEGO
SAN FRANCISCO • SINGAPORE • SYDNEY • TOKYO

Elsevier Butterworth–Heinemann
30 Corporate Drive, Suite 400, Burlington, MA 01803, USA
Linacre House, Jordan Hill, Oxford OX2 8DP, UK

Library of Congress Cataloging-in-Publication Data
Application submitted

British Library Cataloguing-in-Publication Data
A catalogue record for this book is available from the British Library.

ISBN-13: 978-0-7506-7911-4
ISBN-10: 0-7506-7911-5

For information on all Elsevier Butterworth–Heinemann publications visit our Web site at www.books.elsevier.com

Printed in the United States of America
05   06   07   08   09   10   10 9 8 7 6 5 4 3 2 1

In memory of Dorothy E. Deuschl (1917–2004)

Contents

CHAPTER 1
The Travel and Tourism Industry and PR's
Role in It

vii

CHAPTER 2
PR at Hotels and Lodging Establishments

CHAPTER 3
Restaurant Public Relations

Chapter 4
Transportation Public Relations

Chapter 5
Destination and Tourist Attraction PR

CHAPTER 6
What Travel and Tourism Employers Should Understand
About PR

APPENDIX A
Selected Travel and Tourism Professional/Trade Associations
141

APPENDIX B
The Travel Industry's PR Response to 9/11
147

APPENDIX C
Selected Travel and Tourism Print Media
(with circulations over 43,000)
155

APPENDIX D
Selected U.S. Universities Offering Hospitality and Tourism
Education (and Their Concentrations)
159

Preface

Travel and tourism, as this book substantiates, is the economic bedrock of countless communities across this nation. The industry, comprised of disparate sectors, for a long while was quite fragmented. But in recent times these sectors have pulled together to become a most formidable economic force. The most dramatic example of this unity was demonstrated in the wake of 9/11/01 (see Appendix B). Prior to the terrorist attacks that day, travel and tourism was growing steadily. Afterward, the numbers plummeted as the traveling public became apprehensive about its safety and the economy slumped. However, due to prompt post-9/11 measures taken by all of the travel and tourism sectors, and aided by an improving economy, the industry has since made a strong recovery. All of the sectors, except for the airlines, were again operating at near-record levels at the time of publication of this volume.

Public relations (PR) practitioners are widely dispersed throughout the industry's four major sectors—hotels, restaurants, transportation, and destination/tourist attractions—and they have proved in many cases to be very effective, especially in the launching of new services. There are, however, some hospitality managers who seem oblivious to the long-term value of dedicated PR programs. Hopefully, this book will help to enlighten those managers.

The author's inspiration for this textbook came from his recent experience in teaching a noncredit elective course with a similar title in the University of Virginia's (Northern Virginia Center in Falls Church) Public Relations Certificate Program. In the course of his research for the class he discovered: (1) Never before had a class devoted exclusively to the practice of PR in the travel and tourism industry been offered at a U.S. college or university; and (2) there was no available textbook that exclusively focused on the practice *throughout* the industry. With the exception of one 10-year-old text on hotel public relations, which is now out of print, the remaining available textbooks concentrate on marketing and sales promotion techniques, with only brief mentions of the separate discipline of PR and its importance to the industry.

This volume is therefore aimed mainly at undergraduate travel and tourism majors and hospitality managers, with the intent of introducing them to the overall practice of PR and examining how the job is being accomplished today within each of the industry's four major sectors. Hospitality managers, in particular, will learn what PR is and is not, how to hire in-house PR staff or outside counselors, the value of PR to the organization, and what results they can reasonably expect from the practice.

To analyze the practice in the industry's major sectors, the author overlays these traditional communications components on each of the four major industry sectors to identify those components of greatest importance to each sector: PR tools, targeted messages, audiences and media, and crisis communication management. This analysis uncovers an impressive diversity among the four major sectors in terms of PR priorities and techniques.

I am deeply indebted to two individuals, in particular, for providing me with the impetus to persevere with this project and to see it through to its conclusion.

First, my wife, **Vivian Deuschl,** vice president of public relations for the Ritz-Carlton Hotel Co., who supported this undertaking from day one. I relied heavily on her 20 years' experience in nearly every phase of travel and tourism to organize the contents, and on her vast network of industry contacts to identify sidebar contributors and subject-expert reviewers. Vivian's professional perspective was especially valuable in the organization of the hotel PR chapter. Her incredible patience, alone, in editing my first chapter drafts and in furnishing me her candid feedback, deserves this extra recognition.

Second, **Dr. Douglas C. Frechtling,** chair of the George Washington University Department of Tourism and Hospitality Management. It was Dr. Frechtling who so graciously agreed to initially listen to my ideas, who confirmed my research findings that this book would fill a definite void, and who guided me through the rigorous proposal process for publication. From the outset, his enthusiasm for this endeavor never flagged.

Along with learning what PR communications components are of most importance within each major industry sector, readers are given valuable supplementary information in the chapters in the form of sidebars and case studies by the author and by numerous industry PR experts, and in the appendices, which cover a listing of more than 30 selected travel and tourism organizations, a 2003 speech detailing the industry's rapid PR response to the

9/11/01 terrorist attacks on the United States, a listing of selected industry research/statistical sources, a listing of selected U.S. universities offering hospitality and tourism education, and advice on how to organize press trips.

I am also especially grateful to the following practitioners who shared with me their expertise in their respective travel and tourism sectors and who did double duty serving as my subject review experts for the chapters covering their sector specialties, which are designated in the parentheses. They are: **Vivian Deuschl** of the Ritz-Carlton Hotel Co. (Chapter 2, hotel PR); **Wendy Reisman** of the Ritz-Carlton Hotel Co. (Chapter 3, restaurant PR); **Chris Chiames** of US Airways (Chapter 4, transportation PR's airline section); **Brad Ball** of Silversea Cruises LTD and **Christine Fischer** of the International Council of Cruise Lines (Chapter 4, transportation PR's cruise line section); and **Maura Nelson** of the Destination Marketing Association International (DMAI) (Chapter 5, destination/tourist attraction PR).

Finally, my deepest thanks goes out to my 12 sidebar contributors who provided this volume with such extraordinary insights on the chapter subject matter discussed. Their best-practices sidebars provide professional, real-life strategies, advice, and solutions to contemporary PR challenges in all of the major travel and tourism sectors by a virtual *Who's Who* cross section of industry experts.

They are: **Chris Barnett**, airlines, travel, and PR writer for more than 30 years, and co-founder and senior editor of *Bulldog Reporter*, San Francisco; **Jeff Clouser**, former innkeeper, Maytown Manor (Pa.); **Laura Davidson**, president, Laura Davidson Public Relations, New York City; **Vivian Deuschl**, vice president, corporate public relations, the Ritz-Carlton Hotel Co., Chevy Chase, Md.; **Nancy Friedman**, president, Nancy

Friedman Public Relations, New York City; **Geralyn Delaney Graham,** principal, Resources PR, Lawrence Harbor, N.J.; and **Peter Greenberg,** travel editor, NBC *Today Show,* and chief correspondent, the Travel Channel, Studio City, Calif.

Also, **Tom Head,** executive wine and food editor, *The Washingtonian Magazine,* Washington, D.C.; **Vicki Johnson,** communications and development director for sales and travel operations at Walt Disney Parks & Resorts, Orlando, Fla.; **Rudy Maxa,** contributing editor to *National Geographic Traveler,* host and co-executive producer of Public TV series *Smart Travels* and Public Radio's *Savvy Traveler,* and freelance travel writer, St. Paul, Minn.; **Virginia Sheridan,** president, M. Silver Associates, Inc., New York City; and **Jeanne Sullivan,** associate vice president, public relations, Greater Miami Convention and Visitors Bureau.

I am also very grateful to **Dexter Koehl,** vice president, public relations and communications, Travel Industry Association of America, Washington, D.C., for allowing me to reprint his powerful post-9/11 speech as Appendix B in this textbook and for the valuable industry knowledge he shared with me.

Dennis E. Deuschl
University of Virginia

Foreword

When I first arrived at *National Geographic Traveler* I turned my attention to recasting an upfront section lamely called "News & Tips." The name seemed terribly generic, and as I dug into the content I was shocked. This was supposed to be the magazine's enterprising, newsy section. One filled with items that would help travelers save time, money, and hassle. One that actually might break news. And one that the magazine's PR folks might use to get us on television as a relevant source of travel information.

I discovered that "News & Tips" was written by an ex-staffer on the West Coast who was paid a lordly sum to take a shoebox full of press releases each month and regurgitate them as editorial. I was appalled.

"Don't you think," I asked my then staff, "that our competitors are getting the same press releases? This isn't news. We're simply a clipping service for people who want to send us canned sales brochures."

After the chagrin faded, I hired a consumer reporter from *U.S. News & World Report*, and the section, renamed in that first year

"Smart Traveler," has become a respected, consistent source of real news and trends—not warmed-over public relations releases.

This reveals my first point of good PR—don't be obvious and create news. Here are 10 other important observations critical to today's public relations professional working in the travel industry. Some may seem obvious but, judging from my in-box, they bear emphasizing.

We don't work for you. Don't treat a travel publication—and by extension those who work for it—as your mouthpiece. Press releases are helpful but few are chosen. You need to think about what we care about, not what you need to push. The idea that we would rush your release into print is, thankfully, a thing of the past.

Understand, really understand, the publication you're approaching. If you don't know how *National Geographic Traveler* is different from *Conde Nast Traveler, Frommer's Budget Living,* and *Travel & Leisure,* you have a problem. All those magazines have very distinct, well-articulated points of distinction. What works for one probably won't work for another. I'd estimate that 80 percent of the pitches we get are being made to our competitors and to umpteen newspapers and TV outlets and Web sites—all at the same time. We have to differentiate ourselves from others in what is becoming a commodified travel-information society. So do you.

Demonstrate your knowledge of the publication—often. Nothing pleases an editor more than to get an occasional letter simply reacting to a story he or she has run, especially if the note comes without an attached pitch.

Cultivate relationships. The author's wife, who was and still is one of the travel industry's best public relations pros, invited me to lunch about 2 weeks after I landed my position as editor of *National Geographic Traveler*. She had no agenda save that of welcoming me to the city and expressing a hope that I could improve the magazine I had inherited. There was no sales job. Over the years, I'm sure we've mentioned her company many times in the course of our independent reporting. She never once tried to push a story or grind an axe. But I know she's there when I need insight or information. In the cosmic sphere of things, our relationship bears fruit for us both.

Be considerate. Don't e-mail me today about an event that must be covered tomorrow—and, yes, that happened this morning. It shows disrespect and a total lack of understanding reality.

Understand what it is I cover. This goes back to being familiar with the magazine. In our case, we don't send reporters to cover news that will be in tomorrow's paper. We come out eight times a year. We're looking for strategies, trends, tactics, great destinations, and smart ideas. But we have no interest in the latest fare hike by Southwest Airlines—unless it prefigures a trend.

Be realistic. I get 200 e-mails a day and my editors boost our collective tally exponentially. A third are from PR outlets. Almost all are boilerplate ramblings that are not targeted specifically to us. I know half the world is seeing the same thing. Frequently they are addressed "to the editor," an impersonalization to be avoided. They are boring, rote, and frequently contain misspellings. They often ask me to open up attached files, which I've learned to be an enormous time sink (rarely valuable, almost certain to crash my computer).

Don't try to buy us. We receive countless press-trip blandishments weekly. We do take press trips and pay a press rate. We send only staffers. And just to places we're genuinely interested in learning about. And when we go it's to pull together a background file. Stories aren't written based on press trips; if the place warrants coverage based on our report we send a writer and photographer back, on our dime, with instructions to be as anonymous as possible.

Be imaginative. We're looking for great stories, not guidebooky destination pieces. We ask our writers to ask themselves: Why *National Geographic Traveler*? Why now? Why me? And what's the story (not just the place)? The same holds true for public relations professionals. You need to go out on a limb and craft a hand-tooled approach to the publications you covet for coverage. I know it's more work. But we have green-lighted stories based on one-of-a-kind pitches from publicists.

Understand that we value you and we need you. When you act professionally, try to understand us, treat us with the respect you seek for yourselves, and work with us without looking for an immediate return—miracles happen. We answer your phone calls. We listen to your ideas. And we seek your advice. And, who knows, we might just become friends.

Happy pitching!

Keith A. Bellows
Editor in Chief
National Geographic Traveler

I

The Travel and Tourism Industry
and PR's Role in It

The Industry's Scope

Travel and tourism in America has become big business. It is the business of trains, planes, and automobiles. Plus cruise ships, tourist attractions, hotels, restaurants, passenger railroads, motor coaches, tour companies, and much more. These components can be categorized into four major sectors: hotels, restaurants, transportation, and destinations/tourist attractions. Twenty years ago, the business of the industry was generally considered by the media to be "soft" or feature news. It conjured up travel poster images of children frolicking at Disney World, exotic destinations with swaying palm trees, fine dining at sunset, and bathing beauties basking in the sun on white, sandy beaches next to azure blue seas.

These images, of course, still prevail in travel and tourism brochures and advertisements. But today, the press takes the industry much more seriously. A fundamental reason for the change is that industry communicators have succeeded in convincing journalists that travel and tourism has a powerful impact on local and national economies. Stories that once were relegated to feature segments on television and in newspaper travel sections today regularly appear on "prime-time" business news segments and in the business sections of national publications because of the significant economic implications.

For example, the Washington, D.C.-based industry umbrella organization, the Travel Industry Association of America (TIA), points to these impact statistics covering both U.S. resident and international travel in 2003:

Economic Impacts Now Shape Industry News

Travel Expenditures . . . . $554.5 billion
Travel-Generated Payroll . . . . $158.4 billion
Travel-Generated Tax Revenues . . . . . $94.7 billion
Trade Surplus . . . . $2.6 billion
Travel-Generated Employment . . . . 7.2 million jobs

In fact, TIA states on its Web site that travel and tourism ranks as America's third largest retail sales industry, is the nation's largest services export industry, and is one of America's largest employers. (See Appendix A for a list of travel and tourism professional/trade associations.)

In the Washington, D.C. area alone, travel and tourism accounts for 280,000 jobs, making it the area's second largest employment sector, according to city government officials. This area also is the home to nearly all of the industry's major professional and trade associations.

Although most other nations have centralized, federal (usually ministerial-level) travel and tourism agencies, government support of the industry in the United States now comes mainly from the state, regional, and local levels. Up until 1996, there was at the federal level the U.S. Travel and Tourism Administration (USTTA), headed by an undersecretary within the Department of Commerce. That agency, however, was discontinued due to federal budget reductions, and replaced by the Department of Commerce International Trade Administration's Office of Travel and Tourism Industries (OTTI). As a result, major industry promotional initiatives in the United States today are funded and spearheaded by individual industry components such as state travel authorities and city convention and visitor bureaus (CVBs); private, travel-related businesses; and industry professional associations such as TIA.

It should be noted that in 2003 Congress passed legislation creating the U.S. Travel and Tourism Promotion Advisory Board composed of top industry executives to promote travel to the United States. However, the board's initial $50-million funding was subsequently reduced by Congress to $6 million. As of press time for this book, attempts were under way to boost this funding, according to the American Hotel & Lodging Association (AH&LA).

In 1984, the Public Relations Society of America (PRSA) established a new special interest membership section named Travel and Tourism. As of 2004, that section and the newer Food and Beverage section had 683 members, equal to about 3 percent of PRSA's total membership of 20,000. If this figure is indicative of the percentage of the number of travel and tourism practitioners in the total estimated PR population of 200,000 in the United States, there are then an estimated 6,000 travel and tourism practitioners in America. These communicators are well compensated, according to the salary survey in the Feb. 21, 2005, *PR Week,* which said their average salary was $93,239 for professionals in the industry approximately 12 years.

PR TOOLS AND SPECIAL AUDIENCES/PUBLICS

Travel and tourism industry practitioners use all of the traditional PR tools: press releases, press kits, speeches, brochures, pamphlets, exhibits, fact sheets, tours, and special events. Some of the most frequently used industry tools include unedited video footage known as B-roll; extensive computer Web sites; major annual international trade shows such as the International Tourism Bourse (ITB) in Berlin, Germany, the World Travel Market (WTM) in London, England, and TIA's Pow Wow, held in various U.S cities; familiarization or "fam" trips usually for travel writers; media marketplaces; and customer magazines such as *AAA World,* the airline inflights, and *The Ritz-Carlton Magazine*. (See Sidebar 1-1 for a list of standard PR tools and common travel and tourism PR tools.)

The industry's premier annual special event in the United States is National Tourism Week, during the second week of each May. This was established in 1983, when the U.S. Congress passed a joint resolution designating the week. In a White House ceremony the next year, President Ronald Reagan signed a Presidential Proclamation urging citizens to observe the week with "the appropriate ceremonies and activities." Early on, USTTA and TIA took the lead in giving the event a national stage in the capital, but in 1986, industry leaders formed a permanent full-time office at TIA to sponsor the week and expand tourism awareness into year-round programs on the local level across the nation.

In addition to essential audiences such as employees, community leaders, and shareholders, many industry practitioners concentrate their PR efforts on these special publics: meeting planners, tour operators, CVBs, state/regional/local tourism offices, and travel agents. (See Sidebar 1-2, "Travel and Tourism Audiences [Publics].")

SIDEBAR 1-1
STANDARD PR TOOLS AND MOST COMMON
TRAVEL/TOURISM PR TOOLS

STANDARD PR TOOLS:

Press Releases	Frequently Asked Questions
Web Sites	(FAQs)
Publications	Fact Sheets
Special Events	Exhibits
Open Houses	Audiovisuals
Press Conferences	Feature Articles
Video News Releases	Photography
(VNRs)	Letters to Editors
Op-Eds	Speakers' Bureaus
Tours	Statement Stuffers
800 Telephone Numbers	Speeches
Public Service	Radio Actualities
Announcements (PSAs)	CD-ROMs
Editorial Board Meetings	
B-Roll	

MOST COMMON TRAVEL AND TOURISM PR TOOLS:

Press Releases
Fact Sheets
Web Sites
International Trade Shows (ITB, WTM, Pow Wow, etc.)
"Fam" Trips and Press Tours
B-Roll
Custom Publications for Customers
Special Events

SIDEBAR 1-2
TRAVEL AND TOURISM AUDIENCES
(PUBLICS)

Employees
Community leaders
Travel agents
Meeting planners
Guests
Tourists
Diners
Business travelers
Leisure travelers
Luxury travelers
Government officials
Ethnic groups
Special interest
Women
Passengers
Tour operators
Taxi drivers
Suppliers
Stockholders
Customers
Convention and visitor bureaus (CVBs)
State tourism offices
Travel writers
Business
Food writers
Critics/reviewers
Unions
Academia

The travel agent segment in recent years has undergone significant restructuring due to the proliferation of online reservation networks such as Travelocity, Expedia, and Orbitz. These have provided enormous competition for travel agencies—especially in the airline field where all air carriers over the past decade have dropped the 10 percent commissions they used to remit to travel agencies for bookings. These changes have led to the closing of many "mom and pop" agencies and to the consolidation of many others. Still more agencies have had to reinvent themselves by charging service fees, developing niche businesses, and expanding trip advisory services. Agents continue strong relationships with the hotel, cruise line, and tour operator communities. (See Sidebar 1-3 for a list of the ten largest travel agencies.)

FACTORS LEADING TO PR'S PROMINENCE IN THE INDUSTRY

Besides increased business media interest, another major contributing factor to the growing prominence of travel industry PR has been the explosion over the past 20 years of news media outlets dedicated to covering travel and tourism. For example, on cable TV, CNN devotes considerable time to industry news, and now there are cable channels exclusively devoted to travel and food. Every Friday, *USA Today,* America's largest circulation daily newspaper, publishes an extensive travel section, and national newspapers such as *The Wall Street Journal* and *The New York Times* have also expanded their weekly coverage of travel and tourism. In the magazine sector, influential publications such as *Conde Nast Traveler* (circ. 779,081) and *National Geographic Traveler* (circ. 724,119) have emerged as prestigious leaders in industry coverage. (See Appendix C, "Selected Travel and Tourism Print Media.")

SIDEBAR 1-3
TEN LARGEST TRAVEL AGENCIES
(BY SALES IN BILLIONS OF DOLLARS)

1. American Express, Travel, New York, N.Y. $16.0

2. Carlson Wagonlit, Minneapolis, Minn. 12.7

3. Interactivecorp, New York, N.Y. 10.5

4. World Travel, BTI, Atlanta, Ga. 4.2

5. TQ3 Navigant, Englewood, Colo. 4.4

6. Travelocity, Southlake, Tex. 3.9

7. Orbitz, Chicago, Ill. 3.4

8. AAA Travel (AAA Inc.), Heathrow, Fla. 3.0

9. Cedant Travel, Parsippany, N.J. 1.6

10. Liberty Travel, Ramsey, N.J. 1.4

(*Source: Travel Weekly* Power List Web site, Feb. 17, 2005.)

In addition, the following prominent, long-established, industry-wide travel trade and consumer publications help make travel and tourism one of the most well-reported American industries: *Travel & Leisure* (circ. 965,977), *Travel Weekly, Travel Agent Magazine,* and *Business Travel News.* Add to this list publications produced within the industry's four major sectors, regional visitors guides, auto club periodicals, and airline inflight magazines, and we are talking about approximately one thousand publications. (See Sidebar 1-4, "The International Travel Press: The Rules Are Different.")

Giving increased impetus to the proliferation of PR throughout travel and tourism in recent years has been the explosive growth in technology, in particular the Internet and the emergence of hundreds of new channels on cable TV. It used to be that most media outlets worked a typical nine-to-five daily weekday schedule, with only spotty weekend coverage. The changes cited have put many news distribution outlets on a 24/7 schedule.

This has necessitated increased availability of travel and tourism spokespeople as news organizations scramble to fill time and space gaps on an around-the-clock basis.

Another factor contributing to the importance of industry PR has been the urgent need for effective communications management to meet the critical global crises that have arisen in recent years such as the threats of terrorism in the post-9/11 era and the outbreaks of Severe Acute Respiratory Syndrome (SARS) in several nations during 2003. (See Appendix B, "Travel Industry's PR Response to 9/11," and Sidebar 1-5, "10 Ways to Manage Communications in a Crisis.")

SIDEBAR 1-4
THE INTERNATIONAL TRAVEL PRESS:
THE RULES ARE DIFFERENT
BY VIVIAN A. DEUSCHL
VICE PRESIDENT OF PUBLIC RELATIONS
THE RITZ-CARLTON HOTEL CO.

Just because you have had success in placing stories with the travel media in the United States does not mean you can take the same approach when trying to score similar coverage in the growing international travel press. Even countries like Russia and South Korea now have their own editions of glossy lifestyle magazines to appeal to their country's increasingly affluent travelers. This means there is a lot of editorial potential beyond the United States, if you know what the expectations are from the editors and writers on these publications.

If you are planning a press event in a country like **Germany,** it helps to know what the press does and does not respond to in this nation. Don't be surprised after making your announcement and call for questions not to get a single raised hand. This can be awkward and even embarrassing, but it can also be avoided. It helps if you know a particular reporter to ask if he or she will start things off by posing a question. This can evoke a few more so the whole press conference does not seem like a waste of time.

Even better, don't ask for questions and arrange one-on-one interviews after the event, so each reporter can get his or her own "scoop." In Germany, holding a press event in English is acceptable, since most speak and understand English. However, in one-on-one interviews, it is helpful to have someone on hand who can translate the difficult questions from English into German. Make sure you are offering substance, not fluff, and the facts to back up your information. The German travel media are notable for ignoring promotional approaches, instead looking for detail, backed by hard research.

When dealing with the **Asian media,** the same reticence to ask questions at a press conference is not unusual. In this part of the world, especially Japan, the language barrier can be a problem. Any announcements or events in Asian nations, except for Singapore and Hong Kong, require press materials to be translated and for native language speakers to be available at any interviews. This is for your protection—nuances between English and foreign languages can result in a totally different story than anticipated. In the 1980s when the U.S. Travel and Tourism Administration launched a global advertising campaign, it was decided that America would be promoted to foreign visitors by using the slogan "America Catch the Spirit." When translated into Japanese, the words meant something ghostly and the campaign was criticized as being culturally insensitive.

As magazines like *Conde Nast Traveler,* the (U.K.) *Tatler,* and *Travel & Leisure* launch more international editions, a world of new opportunities for promotion of hotels, airlines, cruise ships, and attractions has opened. Many editors are receptive to visits in their offices, as long as PR people come equipped to talk about what is new and different about their product, and the pitch is appropriate to the culture of a country.

As an example, before visiting any of the growing number of travel publications in **the Middle East** to promote a resort spa, be certain your hotel respects the special privacy requirements, including separation of the sexes, that are part of traditional beliefs in Muslim countries. Otherwise, you are wasting your time and have lost credibility in the eyes of this media.

You do not have to travel overseas to promote your travel product to international visitors. Cities including New York, Washington, D.C., Miami, and Los Angeles have large numbers of foreign publications and broadcast outlets with offices and correspondents. While most care about American policies and government coverage, some are also interested in lifestyle news their readers will want to read about before making travel plans. To find a list of such publications, contact the U.S. Department of State (www.fpc.state.gov) in Washington, D.C., and ask if there is a Foreign Press Center in your targeted cities.

When The Ritz-Carlton in Georgetown, Washington, D.C., wanted to let more foreign reporters know about the hotel, they launched a clever food and drink promotion linked to the 2004 infestation of cicadas, a once-every-17-years phenomenon. Called "What's the Buzz in Washington, D.C.?" it featured a creative cocktail and chocolate candies shaped like the insects as a turndown amenity. Correspondents from around the world, stationed in Washington, came to the hotel to film and write about this offbeat but newsworthy feature story.

For PR professionals hoping to improve their international media connections, the Travel Industry Association of America (TIA) hosts "Media Marketplaces" in the United Kingdom and Japan where informal meetings can be arranged in a low-key trade show setting. This is an excellent opportunity to open new doors overseas.

Sidebar 1-5
10 Ways to Manage Communications in a Crisis

Types of Crises

- Accidents, e.g., Three Mile Island, Pa., 1979

- Natural disasters—hurricanes, earthquakes, tornadoes, fires, etc.

- Sudden executive resignations

- Litigation

- Corporate corruption/criminal charges

- Court decisions/lawsuits

- Plant closures/relocations

- Downsizing/layoffs

- Health and safety issues

- Product recalls

- Terrorism

Famous Crises

- Example of Good PR: Tylenol capsule poisonings, 1982

- Example of Bad PR: Exxon Valdez oil spill off Alaska, 1989

CRISIS COMMUNICATION MANAGEMENT STEPS

1. Have a plan or plan annex; annually update, exercise, and train.

2. First 24 hours critical; get CEO to scene ASAP for site inspection & initial press conference.

3. Issue initial statement; show compassion for victims and tell how your organization is responding.

4. Have one designated spokesperson.

5. Have a crisis center and set up action teams.

6. Have prototype news releases ready to fill in and issue.

7. Update corporate Web site with latest crisis info and background info.

8. Set up 800 telephone number for special audiences.

9. Hold daily press briefings near crisis scene. Keep all other key audiences updated daily—employees, environmentalists, and government representatives.

10. Dispatch PR representatives to crisis center and scene, and ensure they all have best telecommunications equipment to speak with each other and to other key organization executives.

What PR Is, and What It Is Not

Since the beginning of modern PR at the start of the 20th century, practitioners have struggled with defining what they do. Several times the PRSA has attempted to have its membership settle upon a concise explanation—without success. To facilitate discussion of the field in this book, the following author's composite definition is recommended:

> *The management staff function that uses truthful two-way communications and operates in the public interest to influence public opinion in order to earn good will and understanding for the organization.*

The PR practice entails the following strategic four-step "RACE" process that was first articulated by John Marston in his book *The Nature of Public Relations:*

R = Research: Surveying existing literature and public opinion.

A = Action: Strategic planning that includes setting objectives, benchmarks, and timelines; message crafting; campaign/program design (including logos and slogans); and budget estimates.

C = Communication: Targeting specific audiences or publics; selecting key messages; identifying the most appropriate news media; and selecting the most effective PR tools and audiences (the principal PR framework for this textbook).

E = Evaluation: Measuring the success of your efforts against the original objectives.

Public relations is both a practice and a profession. It is a practice for all those engaged in its activities. According to the strictest literal interpretation, however, a "PR professional" is a practitioner who is pledged to adhere to a code of ethics dictated by the membership requirements of peer groups such as the PRSA or the International Association of Business Communicators (IABC), and who has been certified by those groups by passing their accreditation examinations. This in no way is meant to imply that practitioners are incapable of producing professional results. They can, and they do, on a large scale. For example, there are approximately 200,000 PR practitioners in America. Of those, however, only an estimated 5,000 of the approximately 20,000 PRSA members have attained professional status by passing PRSA's rigorous written and oral accreditation exams. (See Sidebar 1-6, "In-House PR vs. Outside Agency Support.")

PR Is Not Publicity, Propaganda, Marketing, or Advertising

Public relations is not merely publicity. The latter is a component of the communications step of the practice that is aimed strictly at gaining media attention, while PR encompasses the four-step process of the practice and entails extensive strategic planning and communications to a variety of publics. Another key component in modern PR is aimed at relationship-building with those publics.

Public relations should not be confused with propaganda. The latter involves the manipulation of public opinion through the use of half-truths usually in a controlled or censored environment. By contrast, PR is truth-based and thrives in open societies.

Public relations is also a discipline distinctively different from marketing and advertising. Marketing is totally sales-oriented and concerned mainly with one public—customers. PR is more

Sidebar 1-6
In-House PR vs. Outside Agency Support

In-House PR Staff Advantages

- Most familiar with your corporate culture

- Full-time commitment

- Less expensive

Outside PR Agency Advantages

- More objective

- Specialized services, including:

  1. Media training

  2. Crisis communication

  3. Financial PR

  4. Audiovisual presentations

  5. Speechwriting

  6. Legislative promotion

  7. Corporate ID programs

- Access to nationwide and international offices

- One disadvantage: more expensive. Examples of typical billing arrangements include:

  1. Hourly salary, plus expenses

  2. Retainer for being on call

  3. Fixed project fee

broad-based and embraces many targeted publics. Organizationally, advertising traditionally has been a component of marketing. Advertising is the placement of controlled, paid notices aimed at customers or potential customers, and it lacks the essential credibility that PR messages achieve through the third-party endorsement of the news media.

PR's Rich Hundred-Year Heritage

Modern public relations traces its origins back over 100 years to the dawning of the 20th century. The advent of PR occurred at the height of the Industrial Age in American history. "Big business" was the principal employer of the earliest practitioners—businesses such as America's maturing mining, oil, railroad, and utility companies, which at the time were often confronted with significant labor strife and with the exposure of business abuse scandals in the press.

Between 1900 and 1910 the nation's first PR agencies were established, including one by PR pioneer Ivy L. Lee, who later went on to be PR counselor to oil magnate John D. Rockefeller, Jr. The U.S. Committee on Public Information during World War I turned out to be an ideal training ground for another noted PR pioneer, Edward L. Bernays, who is widely considered "the father of public relations." During the 1920s, Bernays taught the first college-level PR course at New York University, authored the first PR textbook, *Crystallizing Public Opinion,* and articulated the social science foundations for the new practice.

The Great Depression of the 1930s provided the impetus for corporations to seek public support by telling their stories. PR departments sprang up in scores of major companies, and today 5,300 U.S. companies have these departments. Following World

War II, PR experienced explosive growth. For example, the estimated number of U.S. practitioners soared from 15,000 in 1950 to over 200,000 today. The Public Relations Society of America (PRSA) was founded in 1948. Today, that organization boasts a membership of over 20,000.

Based in New York City, the society has 116 chapters across the United States. PRSA's membership participates in 17 special interest sections that include travel and tourism, food and beverage, association, corporate, international, and counselors' academy (agencies). There are also student chapters at 243 colleges and universities that offer PR studies. The society administers a member accreditation program and an annual awards program, oversees professional ethics, operates a professional resource center, conducts various professional development programs, and publishes for members a magazine, newspaper, and electronic newsletter.

MARKETING AND PR SYNERGIES

Despite the sharp distinctions between the two disciplines, the role of PR in the corporate structure often is to supplement marketing efforts. This has proved a very effective alliance in many instances. Regrettably, over the past decade, PR's distinctive identity has become somewhat blurred by the frequent merging of its name into the traditional corporate marketing functions of advertising, pricing, distribution, sales promotion, corporate identification, and demographic research. Prompting this change were the periodic economic downturns that occurred in the 1990s during which PR had a more difficult time justifying its goodwill benefits for companies, compared to marketing's ability to directly demonstrate its contributions to the bottom line. An unfortunate result of this merger activity was marketing's penchant to rename

PR as "marketing public relations" or make PR a part of the newer term "integrated marketing communications."

Looking past this professional rivalry, however, the fact remains that PR's value has intensified since this merger trend with marketing began. For example, in their 2002 book *The Fall of Advertising and the Rise of PR,* branding experts Al and Laura Ries stressed the superior performance of PR versus advertising in launching new products. The fact of the matter is that as part of the marketing environment, PR has given marketing a significant boost in terms of the following factors: building awareness and credibility; holding down sales promotion costs; stimulating sales forces; influencing target groups; and defending products that have encountered public problems. According to a 2004 corporate survey published in the June 28, 2004, edition of *PR Week,* 39 percent of the corporations said Communications/PR reported to the Head of Marketing, compared to 47 percent that said Communications/PR reported to the Chairman/CEO/President.

The remaining chapters of this book are comprised of detailed communications analyses of the four major sectors of travel and tourism—hotels, restaurants, transportation, and destinations/tourist attractions. The final chapter provides practical PR employment advice to top company executives for hiring individual practitioners or outside PR firms/consultants.

ADDITIONAL SOURCES

Bernays, Edward L., *Crystallizing Public Opinion,* New York: Liverright, 1961.

Cutlip, Scott M., Allen H. Center, and Glen M. Broom, *Effective Public Relations,* Upper Saddle River, N.J.: Prentice Hall, 2000.

Gruning, James E., ed., *Excellence in Public Relations and Communications Management,* Hillsdale, N.J.: Lawrence Erlbaum Associates, 1992.

Hiebert, Ray E., *Courtier to the Crowd: The Story of Ivy L. Lee and the Development of Public Relations,* Ames, Iowa: Iowa State University Press, 1966.

Ries, Al and Laura Ries. *The Fall of Advertising and the Rise of PR,* New York: Harper Collins Publishers, 2002.

Seitel, Fraser P., *The Practice of Public Relations,* Upper Saddle River, N.J.: Prentice Hall, 2001.

Tye, Larry, *The Father of Spin: Edward L. Bernays and the Birth of Public Relations,* New York: Crown Publishers, 1998.

Wilcox, Dennis L., Glen T. Cameron, Philip H. Ault, and Warren K. Agee, *Public Relations Strategies and Tactics,* Boston: Allyn Bacon Publishers, 2003.

2

PR at Hotels and Lodging Establishments

Hotels and lodging establishments such as motels, bed-and-breakfasts (B&Bs), and inns make up one of the most labor-intensive sectors of the travel and tourism industry. The primary benchmark of their success is occupancy, or "heads in beds," and a solid average daily rate (ADR)—and PR can strongly influence both. (See Sidebar 2-3, "How to Use PR to Grow an Award-Winning B&B.")

While the majority of hotels do not employ in-house PR staff, most of the larger ones—especially in the luxury category—do have at least one practitioner on staff. For immediate, one-time needs, including grand openings, special events, and crises, hotels often look to their corporate office for specialized PR support, or they turn to outside PR agencies or hospitality consultants for counsel. The determining factor in using outside expertise is usually cost. Whether on a monthly retainer or special project fee basis, outside help can be very expensive. Another downside is that outsiders seldom have a thorough understanding of your corporate culture; however, they often can provide an objective viewpoint that may be needed to meet your PR goals.

The need for professional PR is growing as hotels and their chains diversify their product. Many hotel companies are now involved in "brand extensions." This means they are leveraging their well-respected names to branch out and offer new business-related products, from spas and golf resorts to time-share rentals and private residence ownerships. Such brand extensions require even more intensive PR support involving a group of sophisticated audiences and media that are much more specialized than those in usual hotel PR.

A recent trend among non-hotel companies is to open intimate, "designer" properties in exclusive destinations. These are usually trendy, very expensive boutique hotels that depend on the names of designer companies for their cachet. Armani, Bulgari, and Versace have all recently entered the hotel business with new, highly touted properties around the world. These world-renowned brands, of course, require greater hotel PR expertise and are recognizing that there is a vast difference between promoting fine jewelry and haute couture, and full-service hotels.

PR TOOLS AND AUDIENCES OR PUBLICS

EMPLOYEES

Hotels have a great diversity of audiences that need to be targeted in PR programs. For example, there are employees, with whom you must regularly communicate your messages. Weekly or monthly printed or online newsletters, e-mails, and webcasts are the most common PR tools for these purposes.

Guests

Guests or customers are, of course, a primary audience. The principal PR tools for reaching them are in-room printed collateral, personal letters from the general manager delivered to rooms, printed guest newsletters, and in-room TV programming. In recent years many of the larger hotel chains have launched external consumer magazines aimed at frequent, preferred, and potential guests. The Ritz-Carlton and Four Seasons are two examples of chains that periodically issue lavish publications that carry their name and appeal to upscale guests.

The customer base audience for hotels and the other three major travel and tourism sectors is generally divided into these two categories: leisure and business travel.

Leisure Travel—This category accounts for about 82 percent of all U.S. domestic travel, according to TIA. Most leisure trips are short, lasting one to two nights. Among the most common trip activities are shopping and/or attending a social or family event.

Business Travel—TIA reports that this category accounts for 18 percent of all U.S. domestic travel, generating $153 billion in spending. In 2003, more than 38 million travelers generated 210 million person-trips. The majority of these business travelers are middle-aged men taking an average of seven trips per year. Over half of these travelers fly to their meeting sites if they are 300 or more miles away. Their most sought-after hotel services are Internet access and fitness centers.

Community Groups

Community leaders are another primary audience for hotels because they depend heavily on local services and business tax incentives. Good relations with neighbors is therefore a PR imperative for every lodging establishment in order to demonstrate they are responsible corporate citizens. This is typically achieved through active participation in local civic affairs and charitable endeavors such as the encouragement of employee volunteerism, sponsorship of youth educational and recreational activities, executive participation in civic club programs, and company and employee contributions to local charity fund drives. Marriott International's "Spirit to Serve Our Communities" program, under which employees worldwide donate thousands of hours to support their hometowns, is one notable example of hotel employee volunteerism.

Some of the most commonly used PR tools aimed at communities are press releases to local media, open house programs for the community, and speakers' bureaus that make available hotel executives to address local religious and educational groups. Whatever the form of the hotel's local participation, PR managers should constantly strive to remind the community of the impact their property has on the immediate area in terms of annual taxes paid to local governments, number of jobs generated, the value of contracts with local companies, and the amount of purchases from local suppliers.

SPECIAL HOTEL PR PUBLICS

Several special travel and tourism audiences that hotel PR managers must target because of their direct impact on business are travel writers, convention and visitor bureaus (known as CVBs), meeting planners, and stockholders (if applicable to your corporate structure). (NOTE: While maintaining close relations with travel agents is an absolute necessity for hotels, this normally is not a direct responsibility of the PR manager—it's usually a task assigned to the sales and marketing staff.)

Travel Writers

Travel writers—many of whom are freelancers—are the local hotel PR manager's premier audience. These are the journalists whose first-person accounts have a powerful impact on business. They may visit individually, or be part of press tours or "familiarization (fam) trips." Fam trips are frequently conducted in connection with new openings. While many reporters can no longer participate on these trips because of the complimentary nature of the accommodations and arrangements, some journalists can still attend if a press discount rate is offered. Aside from fam trips, newspapers and magazines, of course, often assign staff members to visit hotels for stories.

In the early days of travel and tourism promotion, PR managers could rely mostly on positive coverage from visiting journalists whose trips were "comped" by hotels. Today, however, many media—especially consumer and general circulation publications—adhere to stricter ethical rules that prohibit the acceptance of complimentary services. The result is that the PR manager now has to work a lot more creatively in attracting and accommodating visiting reporters. Determining which freelance writers will actually be able to generate coverage is a definite challenge.

Hotel PR practitioners attract writers mainly through well-written news releases and creative e-mail "pitches" designed to persuade reporters to visit. For example, you must explain what is so uniquely newsworthy about your property by "painting an irresistible picture" that will especially appeal to the journalist's readers or viewers.

When journalists are in the hotel, the PR manager should be certain that their rooms are furnished with a complete press kit containing information on every detail—from spa hours of operation to facilities for the disabled. A good selection of photography should also be made available on a CD. Early on, the PR manager should meet with writers to review their itinerary and ascertain the story angles they are pursuing so that the manager can arrange appropriate interviews with hotel executives and staff. Some writers like to operate on their own, while others prefer to be escorted throughout their stay.

Travel writers today often specialize in particular "niche tourism" stories, such as ecological or "eco-travel," adventure tourism, gay and lesbian travel, cultural tourism, or family travel. The best way for PR practitioners to identify these niche travel writers is to consult reference books such as the Food, Hospitality & Travel Edition of *Bulldog Reporter's National PR Pitch Book* or directories of the Society of American Travel Writers (SATW).

Convention and Visitor Bureaus (CVBs)

Local convention and visitor bureaus (CVBs) are a second special audience that hotel PR managers must target in their communication strategies. These bureaus are nonprofit marketing organizations that can make hotels aware of potential convention and meeting business (although they usually cannot recommend a specific commercial enterprise). The CVBs are valuable tourist information sources about the local area and frequently are the first point of contact for visiting groups, as well as visiting journalists.

CVBs are often supported by hotel room or sales tax, and are staffed by Chambers of Commerce or local/city governments. CVBs often approach hotel PR managers to partner on press "fams" by hosting rooms or meals.

Depending on their local structures, CVBs in some areas are also called corporations, or centers instead of bureaus. It is imperative that hotel PR managers keep their area CVBs on their news release mailing lists and furnish the bureaus with large quantities of their latest publicity materials.

Meeting Planners

A third very special audience to hotel PR communicators are meeting planners. These are the people directly responsible for booking large blocks of rooms and meeting space for periodic conferences and seminars for the professional and business groups they represent. (Of the audiences mentioned in this chapter, this is the least applicable to most B&B owners and innkeepers, because few of their facilities have sufficient space to accommodate large business groups.) Hotel PR practitioners coordinate closely with the sales and marketing staff in impressing meeting planners when they visit the property in advance of large meetings for customary "site inspections."

Once again, a comprehensive press kit is the most effective PR tool for this special audience. Two large circulation periodicals that are widely read by meeting planners are *Meetings and Conventions* and *Successful Meetings*. These are key media targets that hotel PR managers regularly "pitch" to persuade them to print stories about new angles related to their properties. It is also "good PR" to maintain good relations with the headquarters of Meeting Professionals International, and the American Society of Association Executives (ASAE).

Stockholders

If you are doing PR at the corporate level for a publicly-held hotel company, you have still another key special audience—your stockholders. Reaching this public requires a specially trained and experienced corporate PR practitioner—one who is very familiar with investor relations and all of the federal regulatory requirements regarding the public disclosure of information. Such a person has to deal with a wholly specialized host of financial media, and is very involved in annual report production and communications with financial analysts.

More PR Tools

One PR tool that is fundamental today for all practitioners at hotels—and even the smallest lodging establishments—is the Web site. Most establishments' sites primarily feature sales and marketing information aimed at online reservations by customers. But PR practitioners also have the responsibility of making sure these sites are "press-friendly."

Web Sites, B-Roll, and Special Events

For example, every site home page should have a "press center" option that at the minimum includes PR press contacts and information similar to the contents of a press kit, such as a company profile or fact sheet, biographies of key executives and staff, a brief historical synopsis, copies of the most recent news releases issued, and a file of available photos, with captions, that can be easily downloaded. Web sites today are also vital during crisis communication situations. (See Sidebar 2-1, "Press-Friendly Web Sites.")

"B-roll" is another essential tool that all hotel practitioners should be prepared to furnish to visual media outlets on short notice. This is basically raw, unedited videotape footage of different aspects of your property. It must be professionally shot to ensure usage. You can accompany the footage with a suggested script but TV stations must be allowed to do their own "voice-over." Local TV camera crews will sometimes agree to "trade out" B-roll for rooms. (See Sidebar 2-4, "B-Roll: An Essential, Cost-Effective PR Tool in the Travel Biz.")

Sidebar 2-1
Press-Friendly Web Sites
By Rudy Maxa
Contributing Editor to *National Geographic Traveler*, Host and Co-Executive Producer of Public TV Series *Smart Travels* and Public Radio's *Savvy Traveler*, and Freelance Travel Writer

Looking back, it's surprising the move by travel providers to the Internet took so long.

The airlines made the first move when, in the early 1990s, they launched rudimentary Web sites that allowed anyone with a computer to see where they flew and—if we were willing to work through numerous pages and be patient when our screens froze—even purchase a ticket.

Not only is it hard to remember those days, but it's equally difficult to remember that once upon a time, before the Internet was available to most consumers, booking an airline seat was a cumbersome process made more difficult because there was no easy way to see which airlines flew where and when. We relied on travel agents with their big databases or the kindness of a telephone reservation agent who, if he or she was in a good mood, might share with us the name of competing airlines. Then we could call each of those airlines individually and price fares.

Today, thanks to Web sites that scour the Internet comparing and displaying dozens of fares from a rainbow of airlines, checking prices is about two clicks away on a computer.

Hotel, rental car, and finally cruise companies eventually followed the airlines down the Internet path. Soon, PR professionals realized that Web sites were not only handy for the sales side of a company, but they also could be used to disseminate information to journalists (and interested members of the public) quickly, clearly, and at any hour of the day.

Early efforts on the part of PR folks were pretty clumsy, but the learning curve went up fast. Today, the two paramount goals of a Web site are still the same as when the Internet was a toddler: How do I make my Web site easy and useful?

Here are my rules for accomplishing those twin assignments.

Give Me Information Fast. A home page should be clear about what it offers and how to navigate quickly. Airline home pages often are best at this, appealing both to consumers (who immediately see a grid asking their destination and date and time of departure) and to journalists or others who want to know about a company. One click and most visitors to the site are where they want to be. Terrific. I'm less enamored of hotel Web sites that open with music and dreamy pictures of resorts, especially since some of those lovely displays require downloading software to make them work. If a Web designer simply must set an elaborate scene, at least give me an out—a place to click to skip the froth.

Tell Me What To Do If I Get Stuck. It's surprising the number of home pages—and even entire Web sites—that never provide a telephone number. When I'm Emperor of the Internet, I'll decree that every home page provide a phone number that allows me to reach a live person, as well as the address of the company whose site I'm viewing. As a journalist, I may need a sound bite or quote. Or my questions may not be fully answered on a site. If you're in a business where events may happen after business hours, give me a number of someone to reach, even at three in the morning.

Who, What, Where, When, How & Why. From a PR standpoint, one old-school rule still applies even in the Internet realm: Journalists are still always in a hurry and want a lot of information fast. Posting press releases in chronological order is a good first step. But don't forget to provide a section on a Web site that has all the basics about your company and product. Cut an old hack some slack and let me know in one sentence how to describe your firm. Are you a 42-hotel luxury chain with international properties? Or are you a hotel association with members in North America? Are you a B&B Web site whose members are carefully screened before they're allowed to be posted on your site? Or do you charge a fee for listings and accept all comers?

Change Is Good. The best Web sites are always current. And I mean up-to-the-minute. Your audience—both consumer and media—wants to know the second you are ready to make anything public. If your CEO goes on a morning network television talk show and mentions a new project or sale, the Web site should have details within the hour. That's where the media may go to find the facts for publication or broadcast. And there's nothing wrong with changing the look of a Web site—a favorite past time of Web designers—as long as you keep that home page directory that allows anyone to navigate quickly.

Show Me. If I can't find what I want to know via your home page category listings, give me a search box. And a search box is only as good as the key words it recognizes. So every piece of information that you post on a Web site should be scrutinized and the key phrases or words noted.

Now, you may not work for a travel company. Perhaps you work for a PR firm that deals with travel clients. Have downloadable pictures of your clients' properties or aircraft or cruise ships that an art director can grab for publication, even if it's 8 p.m. and your office is closed.

Let your company's Web site reflect what you do and how I can reach you. List clients. List employees with phone numbers and e-mail addresses. Again, provide after-hours numbers, if appropriate.

And tell me what you can do for me. Do you have a hotel executive who's particularly articulate on hotel trends? A cruise line guru who knows how the industry is changing? Sell 'em on the Web site. Journalists are always looking for experts who can make a complex story simple with authority.

Telling your story is still the bottom line of a PR professional's assignment. Consider the Internet and your Web site as a grand forum, the likes of which both the travel industry as well as the PR profession has never seen before.

Special events are one of the most popular PR tools used by practitioners to gain public attention for their lodging establishments. Many of these events are tied into themes connected with holidays such as Christmas, Easter, Valentine's Day, and Mother's Day, and with community celebrations. For example, an appearance at the hotel by Santa Claus and the Easter Bunny for meetings with the children of guests and local citizens is always a big hit. For the same occasions, hotels with dining rooms will have their chefs design special holiday menus for guests and local events. A more specific example: Every Christmas, one Virginia hotel has gained wide acclaim for annually featuring the World's Largest Gingerbread House, inviting local children to enter and sample a piece of the house. This event is always extensively covered by the media looking for stories with a holiday angle.

Book parties celebrating the publication of new books by noted authors are another special event occasion to consider. Anniversary events commemorating hotel or community milestones can also prove successful. Whatever the event, the hotel PR manager can greatly enhance local news coverage of the event if proceeds from the event can be earmarked for a local charitable cause.

Trade Shows

Finally, for those lodging establishments seeking to attract international visitors and tour operators, one of the most effective PR-marketing tools is participation in one of the major, annual international trade shows such as the International Tourism Bourse (ITB) in Berlin, the World Travel Market in London, and the Travel Industry of America (TIA) Pow Wow, which is held in a different U.S. city each year. At these shows, hotels typically staff a booth that may also include some form of exhibit, e.g., property photos, continuous-loop videotape showing hotel scenes, a model room, etc. All of these shows have pressrooms, where promotional material can be displayed, and one-on-one interviews can be arranged with reporters.

Large amounts of collateral material are kept in the booth, and sales staff stand ready to sign up business from visiting tour operators. The role of the PR manager at these shows is to meet with media reps in attendance to promote the hotel. Ideally, the smart PR manager will arrange to place the company chief executive on the show's master agenda to hold a press conference to make a major news announcement about a new company development.

ABUNDANT MESSAGES/NEWS HOOKS

Besides breaking news stories involving hotels, there are always an abundance of on-site "evergreen" stories, or timeless features; every employee is a potential story. For example: the immigrant housekeeper from Vietnam who has endured great hardships prior to becoming a model American citizen; the affable bartender who is on a first-name basis with many guest celebrities; the resourceful concierge who has gone out of his way to overcome a guest's angst over misplacing an important personal item; a world-renowned chef who is creating exciting new culinary delights in the hotel restaurant; or the security director who is a former military hero.

Another clever feature story idea incorporates the use of animals in hotel promotion. Several establishments have done this so successfully that their animals have actually become an integral part of their brand identification. Notable examples include: the famous lobby fountain ducks of the Peabody Hotel in Memphis, Tenn.; the pair of Dalmatian dogs that roam the premises at The Inn at Little Washington in Virginia; and the Ritz-Carlton, Bachelor Gulch, in Beaver Creek, Colo., where "Bachelor," a white

Labrador retriever, is a hugely popular star of the hotel's Loan-A-Lab Program.

The feature ideas here are, of course, in addition to the typical hard news "hooks" that arise at nearly all lodging establishments such as: facility renovations; new general managers and chefs; innovative room amenities and technological improvements; the inauguration of new, specialized services, e.g., "technology butlers" and "firewood concierges"; special rate packages; culinary creations by the chef or cooking demonstrations for guests and/or local citizens; hotel anniversary observances; on-location shoots by movie or TV shows; spring cleaning tips by the housekeeping staff; or "A Day in the Life" stories where a journalist follows along the general manager or concierge as they perform their varied duties on a typical workday. (See Sidebar 2-2, "Grande Lakes, Orlando—Redefining the Orlando Experience.")

Press interest in guest celebrities or VIPs is always very keen, but these occasions require special handling by the PR manager. The overriding concern of most lodging establishments is maintaining the right of privacy of their guests. As tempting as it might be to let the press know your property is accommodating famous rock music stars, the PR manager must exercise restraint and respect the stars' requests for anonymity, unless they indicate otherwise. The hotel has the right to have its security staff bar the media from the premises so that the hordes do not disrupt other hotel guests. This of course requires considerable tact on the part of all employees.

Stars and Diamonds

A major hard news story that hotel PR managers always tout vigorously is the receipt of major industry awards. None are more prestigious than the annual "star" and "diamond" ratings

Sidebar 2-2
Grande Lakes Orlando — Redefining the Orlando Experience
By Laura Davidson, President
Laura Davidson Public Relations, New York, N.Y.

Situational Analysis: How newsworthy is another hotel opening in the nation's #1 tourist destination, especially if it's not connected to a popular theme park? That was the situation facing Grande Lakes Orlando, a 500-acre luxury resort, which opened on July 1, 2003, and its PR agency, Laura Davidson Public Relations. The $600-million property, the largest non-gaming resort to open [in 2003] in the U.S., features a 584-room Ritz-Carlton and a 1,000-room JW Marriott as well as a Ritz-Carlton managed spa and 18-hole golf course.

There were numerous challenges facing this mammoth project: (1) Orlando is not seen as a luxury destination; (2) The hotel industry was in an economic slowdown and Orlando already had an inventory of 120,000 rooms; (3) This was the Orlando debut for both these brands and the awareness of the JW Marriott was low: (4) Concern toward linking a Ritz-Carlton and Marriott (Marriott owns both brands) on one estate.

Statement of Objectives: Starting one year out, the objectives were: to get coverage in the critical meetings publications. As this resort was creating 1,200 jobs, it was key to penetrate the local and regional media to create excitement in the community and to create a buzz nationally among consumer media. PR needed to redefine Orlando as a viable "luxury" destination and communicate the story of one destination resort with two separate properties. Finally, in the critical two to three months before opening, the goal was to generate advance bookings for the summer (not Florida's peak time).

Program Planning and Strategy: Research was conducted on the Orlando tourism and hospitality market and the luxury travel segment in general to ensure Grande Lakes was not perceived as "just another resort opening." PR began one year prior to launching this resort locally, regionally, and nationally.

Editorial Advisory Board: Created an editorial advisory board consisting of top editors representing the travel, food, and hotel trade sectors. This was to provide insight on the needs of the luxury traveler.

Unique Services: Recognized there was a need for unique offerings at a luxury level—resort created the world's first Citrus Consultant, first Golf Caddie-Concierge program, first Golf Fore Kids Etiquette class.

Key messages: Keeping in mind that this was a huge project with many players and many components, key messages were created to ensure a consistent "voice" when speaking with the media.

Media visits: Arranged pre-opening site tours for meetings, hotel trade, local press as well as consumer media such as the *Miami Herald* to give them a "sneak peek" into what was to come. Helicopter rides were offered as a memorable way of getting a bird's-eye view of this huge resort.

Press releases: Throughout the pre-opening period, communicated information on several different aspects of the resort such as the spa, golf, as well as the special services provided.

B-roll satellite uplink: Combined construction footage along with pre-opening shots and aerial views.

Press kit: Communicated that Grande Lakes will elevate Orlando as a luxury destination with its many high-end services and amenities (such as golf and spa) for the sophisticated traveler.

Results: From TV coverage communicating the hiring effort for 1,200 jobs to the anticipation of the opening, Grande Lakes Orlando was featured in top outlets in all targeted media categories. Orlando's leading paper, the *Orlando Sentinel,* ran a cover story relaying the excitement and positive implications to the local economy. On opening day, all local media stations (including NBC, ABC, and CBS affiliates) broadcast live. National media—CNBC (4 min., 40 sec. segment) and CNN *Headline News*—also covered the debut. In total there were thirty-one broadcast hits.

Other highlights include: *The New York Times, Atlanta Journal Constitution, Los Angeles Times, Miami Herald, The St. Petersburg Times, Time Magazine, American Way,* and *Child.* All leading meetings and hotel trade publications, e.g., *Successful Meetings, Meetings & Conventions, Business Travel News, Hotels, Travel Agent,* featured the resort. In total, the campaign netted an ad value of over $1 million (more than 7 times the PR budget) and a total print circulation/viewership of approximately 53 million. According to Marriott, the opening was "an outstanding success." All key messages were communicated, which was critical in the pre-opening and opening period. The opening was so successful that Grande Lakes Orlando was sold out in its first weekend of operation and the overall summer occupancy exceeded expectations.

of, respectively, Exxon Mobil and the American Automobile Association (AAA). The most sought-after ratings are five stars or diamonds, representing the very best lodging establishments, spas, or restaurants, in terms of available facility amenities, cleanliness, and quality service. The ratings are based on anonymous inspections by company teams. Earning one of these awards can provide a property with huge business advantages. Even though the ratings organizations inform award recipients months ahead of the official announcement, PR managers cannot publicize the honor until Mobil and AAA make the announcement. After that, full publicity to all audiences is appropriate. These awards are so important that if a property receives a downgraded rating, PR managers must prepare in advance to explain reasons for the downgrading in order to avoid negative media stories.

Trade Media Targets

In addition to the many travel media targets cited in Chapter 1, the lodging industry has a bevy of high-circulation trade publications toward which local PR managers should aim their communications. Among the largest monthly trades are: *Successful Meetings* (circ: 72,050), *Meetings & Conventions* (circ: 70,038), and *Hotels* (circ: 62,000). A large semimonthly trade is *Hotel & Motel Management* (circ: 53,386), and another industry trade publication printed thirteen times a year is *Lodging Hospitality* (circ: 50,400).

Hotel Crises Communication

Hotels and lodging establishments encounter crises of various sizes on a daily basis, and these are critical events in terms of overall communications efforts. Nothing can be more damaging to property reputations than mishandled crises. Preparation is the key, and local PR managers must play a prominent role in planning for these mishaps and executing effective communications. Most important is that the PR practitioner be available and thoroughly involved from the beginning. See Sidebar 1-5, "Ten Ways to Manage Communications in a Crisis"; every practitioner should have a written plan that incorporates these guidelines.

Nearly every crisis will necessitate a statement from the general manager that should be issued to all key audiences, especially employees, guests, and the media. A comprehensive crisis plan will address all of these worst-case scenarios: accidental guest deaths; murder/rape/ assault and battery; natural disasters; negative health inspections; celebrity crises; establishment deflaggings or ownership changes; lawsuits; ownership foreclosures; civil unrest and terrorism threats; room cleanliness; downgraded ratings; owner issues; and employee problems, executive misconduct, and labor union unrest.

BED-AND-BREAKFAST (B&B) PR

The practice of PR at B&Bs can be especially educational because it demonstrates "grassroots hotel PR" at its most fundamental level. Newcomers to the practice can witness many of the standard PR tools, messages, media targets, and audiences in operation on the smallest possible scale.

Across the United States there are about 20,000 licensed B&Bs and country inns, representing 170,000 rooms, according to the Professional Association of Innkeepers International (PAII). Half of these properties operate in small towns, 32 percent in very rural locations, and the balance in urban areas. (The primary customer base for B&Bs is leisure travelers, as opposed to most hotels and motels that have sizable meeting room space and which depend on a mix of leisure and business travelers.)

Many B&Bs are "mom and pop operations" managed by family members. It is not unusual for innkeepers to assume multiple operational roles such as general manager, concierge, bellhop, housekeeper, server, *and* PR manager.

Basic PR tools for the typical B&B startup include simple brochures and flyers, press releases, and Web sites. Innkeepers often employ local freelance talent to develop these tools. Most new property owners concentrate their media relations on potential local guests, and local and regional press outlets within a 200-mile radius of their establishment. The owners frequently take on the responsibilities of principal media spokesperson, escorting journalists through their property and befriending local editors and reporters.

Because innkeepers must focus their PR efforts on local goodwill and patronage to sustain their businesses, it is essential for them to also maintain close liaison with their local convention and visitor bureaus and state tourism offices to promote their properties beyond the immediate market area. Participation in community betterment and civic activities, of course, is also a must.

Typical B&B media messages include the following: portraying their properties as romantic getaways, and as rest stops in close proximity to a range of exciting tourist attractions; announcements about new menu items, special services and amenities; and building improvements and historical facts connected to the home or inn. Many B&Bs maintain visitor ledgers in which guests write candid comments, and these often provide interesting copy for the local media.

SIDEBAR 2-3
HOW TO USE PR TO GROW AN AWARD-WINNING
BED & BREAKFAST (B&B)
BY JEFF CLOUSER, INNKEEPER
MAYTOWN MANOR B&B
MAYTOWN, LANCASTER COUNTY, PA.

(NOTE: In 2000, Jeff converted a private, historic federal-style residence in the heart of Pennsylvania Dutch Country into a highly successful B&B—primarily through the application of sound PR and marketing practices. His B&B was the 2004 winner of *Arrington's Inn Traveler* "Most Hospitality Award," the 2003 winner of *Arrington's B&B Journal* "Best Breakfast Award," and the 2002 second-place winner of *North American Inns Magazine* "Room of the Year Award." In late 2004, Jeff sold Maytown Manor.)

I think these are some of the factors that have contributed to our PR/Marketing strategies for Maytown Manor Bed & Breakfast in Maytown, Lancaster County, Pa.

A. Research B&B industry by actually staying at B&Bs for three years before opening our own inn. Making notes of what we liked or didn't like as guests so we knew what to include in our B&B.

B. Read books such as *So You Think You Want to be an Innkeeper*, join professional associations such as Professional Association of Innkeepers International (PAII), and subscribe to trade magazines such as *Arrington's B&B Journal*, *Inn Traveler*, and *Yellow Brick Road*.

C. Attend seminars such as Inn Deep Workshop for Aspiring Innkeepers in Cape May, N.J., or attend Small Business Development Classes at a local college, or actually intern at a B&B.

D. When opening a B&B think about location, type of guests you want—leisure vs. business—which dictates the type of amenities, décor, and marketing you will do for your B&B. How many rooms do you want and can you get help to assist at the inn? Will you accept children or pets, will you allow smoking, and will you be handicapped accessible? What is your niche?

E. As you prepare to open, start to network with Chambers of Commerce, visitor bureaus, and business associations. Join the local B&B association and get to know your local innkeepers. Begin Internet presence with an easy-to-navigate and informative Web site. Make sure you exchange links with local attractions and include pictures on your site. Don't forget to contact local press about your grand opening and have an open house for the public and for local businesses. Perhaps you could host a Chamber Mixer at your property.

F. The amenities in your B&B can help with PR. Embossed soaps with B&B info; embossed toilet paper with B&B info; postcards/notepaper and pencils/pens with B&B info; handing out Pennsylvania state maps with B&B info; giving gifts to guests for special occasions such as a jar candle or your cookbook with B&B information; selling B&B items in your gift shop; providing self-service guest pantry for snacks, drinks, and ice; providing robes, rooms with private baths, good mattresses, high thread count sheets, turndown service with mint on pillow, excellent breakfasts, great customer service—all this should keep your guests talking once they leave your inn.

G. Don't be discouraged, it takes years to build your business and get established with new and repeat guests. Keep in mind what can affect travel. We opened in a year when the economy was not so good, then 9/11 happened, and now we have high gas prices. Travel is affected by outside factors such as these but hang in there. Lucky for us our business did increase every year with our fourth year hitting a plateau.

H. Once established, join state B&B associations, attend seminars for B&B owners, network with fellow innkeepers via these seminars or chat rooms, become active in marketing with local B&B associations and business associations. I sought training in customer service/front desk procedures and earned my Food Safety Certification. Make sure you let the press know about these accomplishments and include them in your brochure, mailings, and on your Web site.

I. Go after press—invite travel writers, respond to travel writers' requests for information on such things as spas or wineries if you have those things in your area. Seek out recognition for your B&B and let the press know when you receive an award either through local press or such sites as www.prweb.com. Do things that will attract press coverage such as a house tour for charity or sponsor a fundraiser for a local organization in need such as the local library. Let the press know what guests are saying about your B&B through your in-room guest diaries or on sites such as www.tripadvisor.com.

Sidebar 2-4
B-Roll: An Essential, Cost-Effective PR Tool in the Travel Biz
By Peter Greenberg
Travel Editor, NBC TV's *Today Show*, and Chief Correspondent, The Travel Channel

I started out as a print journalist, as the West Coast correspondent for *Newsweek*. I worked with limited copy space, and limited time (we were, after all, a newsweekly). And my challenge each week was to report stories in which I could in short order explain the story, keep it balanced, and equally important, set the scene, paint as much of a realistic picture as possible. If I was successful, the readers would be able to relate to the story and then, based on the information I gave them and the images I presented, make reasonably intelligent decisions and choices.

That's what good reporting and writing is all about—getting people information in a way that is acceptable to them, gives them the news they can use, and gives them enough information with which to digest ideas, and then decide.

Then, about 20 years ago, I took on another title, that of television broadcast journalist, and I had to make some large adjustments in the way I painted those pictures.

The assumption is that you're working on a good story, but no matter how colorful the writing, how poignant the story points, how powerful the message, it's... television. And television is unforgiving when it comes to visual support. For a magazine, much of the visual support is in the writing, in the painting of those pictures.

But with television, if there's no good video, then there *is no story*. It's as simple, and as direct as that.

No one watches me on television to see what I'm wearing or to learn who I'm dating. They watch me because they want information. Travel has become the largest industry in the world. It employs the most number of people, and is singularly responsible for the GNP of more than 80 countries. Without travel and tourism, their economies would be paralyzed and falter.

B-Roll vs. "The Brochure Mentality"

The travel industry has always depended on visual support— but that visual support is often misguided, and ultimately misleading. It is a brochure mentality in which almost every word ends in "est." (best, greatest, finest, etc.) and where the visual support is equally troublesome. The people featured in these brochures come in three distinct and disturbing categories: breast enlarged women at the pool toasting wine glasses; Ken and Barbie in their dress whites on the tennis court, or the two hardest working folks in the brochure industry: the senior couple in their bathrobes, standing on their balcony and gazing out at... well, no one knows, and no one cares.

This brochure mentality might still work for those travelers, or perhaps I should say tourists, who are "unevolved" and actually think the world is populated by Size 2 women. The brochure mentality might even work for those who truly believe that every beach is pristine, every restaurant deserves the words "fine dining," and the sun sets beautifully every evening.

Of course, most travelers know that brochures, almost by definition, are misleading. However, the problem is compounded exponentially when those in the travel industry use the same philosophy to produce videos to support their products.

Sales and marketing people have been trained, conditioned, and ultimately behave to *promote* their products. Most have yet to learn how to *present* them.

Television journalists need good quality B-roll—video footage to visually support many of the stories they are reporting, especially round-up stories. It is highly unlikely that a television network, let alone an affiliate, would commit a camera crew to spend a full day getting video just to be able to use 20 seconds for one of their stories. And yet, that 20 seconds of video is what broadcasters need, and what publicists dream of having on network, syndicated, and local news.

And therein lies the problem. The travel industry is about 20 years late when it comes to television. Travel is news, and yet the travel industry still sees travel reporting as nothing less than an advertising vehicle. When video does exist, it is nothing less than fluff, and bad fluff at that. It is promotional video with those breast-enlarged women, Ken and Barbie, and the color-coordinated senior bathrobe couple. Or, it's a sales and marketing video, with slick edits, narration, and music, that is also unusable. A useless video brochure that is, more or less, a caricature.

If you ever see me hold up a slide on any of my television venues, it will likely be my last appearance there. And, if I use sales and marketing video, it is most often to visually illustrate a promise a hotel, airline, or cruise line has made that it hasn't kept.

Since so much of the public relations component of any business, and in particular travel, is justified by "impressions," "inches," and equivalent advertising value, the argument for good, quality, *real* B-roll is made even more compelling when you look at the numbers.

A five- or six-day B-roll shoot, not counting transportation, averages between $30,000 and $50,000. A 20-second advertisement on the *Today Show,* for example, can cost in excess of $180,000. Average times for segments on the *Today Show* run about 4 minutes. The math equation is easy to figure out.

And yet the majority of the travel industry still resists shooting network quality B-roll to support the very stories and experiences it desperately wants to sell. One of the reasons, perhaps, is that within the labor structure of a hotel, cruise line, or airline, video budgets are controlled by sales and marketing, not public relations. And sales and marketing wants to use video to make even more brochures, to make everything even more pretty; it's that ridiculous.

It's unnecessary, misleading, and unfortunate too.

Recent history indicates that when those in the travel industry have identified good stories and experiences, and then hired professional, network freelance camera crews to shoot B-roll to support those stories; when they haven't interfered in the shooting process to try to beautify or "food style" the shots; their batting average of getting those stories on the news has been exceptionally high. And the audience reaction has been immediate, and tangible.

That requires a specific budget as well as a specific vision. The hotel, for example, that hires the crew is not hiring them to shoot one story, but to shoot tape that supports numerous possible stories, ranging from great travel programs for kids, unusual hotel services, handicapped accessible travel, educational travel, hotel crime, hotel safety and security, et al. Not one tape, but many 4- and 5-minute natural sound tapes that are not edited, but shot by these freelance news crews in a way that makes them easy to edit. No sound or camera effects, no narration, no marching bands. No models. Real people doing real things.

Shooting B-Roll for Network TV

It is important to hire an experienced, network freelance news crew. Not a promotional production company. Too often, hiring of crews is based on transportation cost, and local crews are hired instead. And while there are many very good local crews, most do not know how to shoot for the networks. And the results are disastrous.

Sometimes, when television stations arrive to shoot a story and have their own crews, attempts will be made to do a trade-out with these local stations—hotel rooms, meals in exchange for free use of their video. Almost always, this doesn't work for the same reasons as hiring a local crew—and in some cases, the video that is released is carrying the "bug" or the I.D. of the initial shooting network or channel on the lower right of the screen. Translation: unusable footage.

But, using the hotel example—if the right crew is hired, if stories are identified and shot as individual stand alone B-roll tapes, the upside is great. First, since the hotel owns the tapes as well as the masters, it can then do an additional edit, and create an effective sales and marketing tape, thereby killing two birds with one stone. And, unless there is a dramatic change in the hotels' design, or the programs, in most cases, this B-roll has a shelf life of at least two, if not three years.

And second, tape duplication is inexpensive, and suddenly the PR folks who represent the hotel have much needed visual support and ammunition. They can then pitch stories that are no longer in a vacuum. A producer at an affiliate or a network that gets a story pitch AND great supporting video is more likely to go with the story.

I am NOT talking about a self serving VNR, or video news release, featuring a boring talking head, usually appealing only to the ego of the executive interviewed who was also the one who was talked into shooting it in the first place.

I am talking about usable, real footage.

And then, when you do the math, one network use justifies the entire expense of the original shoot. But if it's a good story, you'll get multiple hits over a period of 18 to 36 months on numerous networks, syndicated shows, and network affiliates as part of their local news coverage.

Sadly, most in the travel industry have yet to figure this out. And as a result, a majority of those in the travel industry who have a great product or great experience are still not on television.

It is a very simple solution. If you amortize the cost over 18 or 36 months, and also incorporate the real potential for also converting the B-roll into dual use as sales and marketing video, it becomes a no-brainer.

One clarification: I say this not as your marketing partner (because I am definitely not), but as someone who is constantly in search of good stories for my audience. And, as a journalist who still believes he knows good stories when he hears them, I'd like to think I'll also be able to see them. And so would my audience.

3

Restaurant Public Relations

Of all the major sectors of travel and tourism, restaurant PR requires some of the most specialized knowledge and language. This, and the fact that nearly half of all new restaurants fail in their first few years and the viability of a restaurant is heavily dependent on the critical reviews it receives, present unique high-risk challenges for the PR practitioner.

In the hotel sector, restaurants are often a necessary amenity—but they seldom are big revenue producers. Rarely will you find a hotel restaurant supported by a dedicated restaurant PR practitioner. Instead, an outside PR consultant or agency will most likely be employed. The latter type of PR support is very common for individual, free-standing restaurants—especially for the purposes of creating an initial "buzz" or word-of-mouth popularity during a restaurant's first few months of operation.

Different classes of restaurants have different PR audiences, tools, and messages. For example, fast-food chain restaurants have very large, geographically dispersed operations in terms of employees and corporate structure. With greater employee numbers, the chains use the traditional communication tools such as online and printed newsletters, individual recognition programs, and webcasts.

Fast-Food vs. Individual Restaurants

A key audience for chains such as McDonald's is their respective communities. They communicate with their communities through sponsorships of local educational and recreational projects involving neighborhood youths and through participation in other local events. McDonald's "Golden Arches" logo is recognized globally, as is their "spokesclown," Ronald McDonald. One community relations effort that earns them extensive good will is their Ronald McDonald House program, which provides temporary lodging for the families of sick children who are being treated by area hospitals.

Most of the fast-food chains have incorporated their proven PR and marketing techniques into standard operational procedure packages, which individual restaurant owners agree to implement when they purchase a franchise.

In contrast with these chains, individual restaurants must establish their own brand identities. They, too, put a high value on good community relations, but their PR focus is primarily on their dining audiences and food writers. Some of their key tools are B-roll, a Web site, menus, press releases and press kits, and participation in special events such as theme dinners, wine tastings, chef guest appearances, cooking classes, wine tastings, and food festivals. (See Sidebar 3-1, "Restaurant Openings and Beyond: Tips for Creating and Continuing the Strong Buzz.")

SIDEBAR 3-1
RESTAURANT OPENINGS AND BEYOND:
TIPS FOR CREATING AND CONTINUING
THE STRONG BUZZ
BY GERALYN DELANEY GRAHAM, PRINCIPAL
RESOURCES PR, LAURENCE HARBOR, N.J.

The launch of a restaurant is a magical time. Unlike a retail product that is manufactured and packaged, the opening period of a restaurant is a live, organic process, with continuous tweaking to details of the food and service through the first few weeks. So timing plays an important role in the public relations plan for a restaurant launch. You want to create a strong opening buzz, yet give the clients enough time to refine those details that can give their restaurant that extra star in their review.

In New York City, where everything happens in a compressed time period, this can be a tricky game. In all cases, I advise that you communicate directly with the owner, service director, and chef of the restaurant. They will know when they are ready to "go," or if they need a week or two of "soft opening" phase before opening the publicity flood gates.

There are two distinct phases to any restaurant opening:

1. The *Launch Phase,* which lasts from four to six weeks prior to opening to about three to four months after the opening day. It includes all of those important opening announcements in print, Web, and electronic media in both local and national outlets that will drive diners in your client's doors as well as the various critical reviews that all restaurants want and need to sustain their business.

2. The *Ongoing Phase* is where the real creative process of developing and pitching story ideas happens. The goal is to create a series of consistent placements in varied media so that different demographic groups can learn about your restaurant. For example, while it is definitely important to have client coverage in the dining/food section of your local newspaper(s), it is equally important to be included in related articles in the business and style sections. Other key media include travel, women's, and men's lifestyle magazines and Web sites, as well as regional magazines like *New York Magazine* or *D Magazine* (in Dallas) and healthy eating magazines like *Cooking Light*.

Of course, there is an overlap between the two phases where your PR team begins to research and develop these stories while the Launch Phase is still the focus. I have found that the best story ideas are created when you really know the product—in this case, the menu (and interesting ingredients or techniques on that menu), interesting aspects of the service and the wine/cocktail list, and great stories about the chef, as many writers like to focus on their interests, activities, and recipes.

THE LAUNCH

The Goal: Create the buzz, get the word out, and pique the food critics to come in and review the restaurant.

The Process:

1. *Know your product*. You can't publicize a product you haven't eaten, so make sure you try the food (preferably more than

once!) before the restaurant opens. Understand its ingredients, and know why the organic roasted chicken from Stone Church Farm is so special or if that delicious goat cheese made by Trappist monks is being served in any other area restaurants. In other words—do your homework! Talk to the chef, the sommelier if there is one, and the service director—they are a wealth of interesting information for your press release and for future story ideas! Clarify what makes your client distinctive and unique from others—find your "hook."

Example: Gaia restaurant in Greenwich, Connecticut, had signature dishes on its menu that were cooked in mason jars—yes, like ones your grandmother made jelly and preserves in. In order to learn about the process and how to publicize it as a credible product rather than a gimmick, I spent hours talking to the chef and a morning in the kitchen with him learning the cooking process, which is based on age-old cooking methods. This knowledge empowered me to answer questions from press and I created a credible everything-old-is-new-again technique story that was written about in national media outlets.

2. *Create an impressive press kit.* There will be a day when we can send all press kits via e-mail or CD, but it hasn't arrived yet. Many top writers still prefer a hard copy of the kit, even if they like to get a preliminary announcement and basic facts via e-mail.

Words are important, and writers and editors appreciate a well-written kit. The press kit should include:

- Fact sheet.

- Bio on chef, pastry chef, and owner (optional).

- A really great press release that describes the philosophy or the concept of the restaurant, the food, the décor, and any other significant aspects—for example, the wine list or the service style.

- Menus/wine lists.

- Special details page: If there is something new or unique about this restaurant, consider developing a special one- to two-pager about it.

Example: For the opening of the much-awaited Jean Georges restaurant in New York, Chef Jean-Georges Vongerichten designed his four-star menu to include wild edible plants (herbs and weeds) to season his dishes. We created a two-page piece with illustrations and written descriptions of the plants and how Jean-Georges was using them on his menu. This was the first time this had been done in the United States and even food writers weren't familiar with yarrow and lamb's quarters and wood sorrel, and the feedback on this piece was very enthusiastic—*The New York Times* wrote a two-page feature article on a day foraging with the chef and included recipes of easy-to-cook-at-home dishes.

Package the kit to reflect the décor or philosophy of the restaurant. Make it as pretty to look at as it is to read—use different kinds of colored or textured paper to jazz it up if appropriate. Work within the client's budget—you don't need a huge budget to develop a stunning-looking kit.

Tip: Find a website like www.paperaccess.com or a local specialty store to use as your resource for great looking press kit packages. Many restaurants don't have the printing of stationery as a priority for their opening, so be prepared to create a letterhead and press kit shell for them. Use PDF files of your client's logo to create letterhead and stickers for the kit. Mock up two "looks" for the client to review, along with a budget for each.

3. *Get on the phones and online.* After you have your fact sheet and bio of the chef written, release information to targeted press who write opening pieces. This should be a brief release or media alert, a teaser almost, but it is good to have the fact sheet and chef bio as an attachment to an e-mail or fax.

4. *Send out your press kits.* Send the kits to local, national, and freelance press in the food, wine, travel, and lifestyle areas.

Tip: Develop a good network of freelance writers to work with. I have found that these writers, who have to pitch story ideas constantly in order to make a living (see, they are just like us!), are very open to new ideas and information. Be good to them, and they will be good to you—and your clients.

5. *Get the food press in your restaurant to EAT!* Unlike other products that can be sent via mail for the media to examine and try on their own, with restaurants it is often necessary to get the writers and editors in to experience your client's food and atmosphere before they will write about it in depth. There are two ways to do this—invite writers in individually to dine, preferably with you or another account executive, or plan a media dinner.

Tip: How to Plan a Great Media Dinner: Make beautiful invitations. Hold the dinner on two different nights and give the media their choice of date so that they have two opportunities to work with their very busy schedules. Keep table sizes intimate—six to eight persons maximum—and have a representative from your agency or the restaurant host each table.

If you are trying to get press to a location that is out of reasonable travel distance, make it easy and fun for them (see the following Example). Always send them home with a little gift bag of something delicious for them to snack on the next day. They will be reminded what a wonderful time they had at the restaurant.

Example: When I plan a New York City-based editors' and writers' dinner for my clients in the tri-state area of New Jersey, Connecticut, or upstate New York, I hire a limo or executive van to drive the press back and forth. Then I have the cocktail hour in the car—with a wonderful, interesting vintage of Champagne and finger-snack foods prepared by the chef to munch on. It saves time, helps breaks the ice, and if there is traffic (ugh!), a good bottle of champagne helps pass the time a little more quickly.

ONGOING PUBLICITY

Once your client has their opening announcements and review out, it is time to begin the process of *keeping* your client in the press. Here are a few of our favorite tips to obtain this goal:

Don't Rely on Generic Press Releases for a Story

Use press releases and media announcements to announce general information like holiday events, awards, and seasonal menu highlights to a larger group of media. But to place a custom feature story, it is better to create a story idea, then match it to a targeted publication/Web site/TV show. Then you pitch it to a specific writer who you know has interest in that kind of story. Have two alternative targets/writers for the story in case your first choice isn't interested or the timing is wrong. If it gets turned down three times, then you need to come up with a new idea.

Watch for Trends in Dining

If you see a new ingredient being used by your client and at least two other restaurants—you have a trend. Pitch it as a recipe-driven story. *Never* hesitate to use non-client restaurants to obtain a placement for your client—having your client in part of the story is better than no placement at all. In addition, the writer will appreciate your efforts and it adds to the credibility of the trend.

Learn the Ins and Outs of TV Pitching

- There are different rules for TV, and producers change constantly, so it is good to have a person in your office be the designated "TV pitcher." Some things to keep in mind:

    - Smaller, local stations are a good stepping stone for your chefs to test their TV presence, and local stations are usually happy to have a local personality appear live for a cooking demonstration.

- Network affiliates and cooking shows on Food TV or similar usually require a tape of your chef cooking live (this is where the small local stations are helpful).

- National shows like *The Today Show* usually need a national tie-in—i.e., a chef who owns restaurants in various U.S. locations or a restaurant/chef that has just come out with a cookbook.

- If you have a chef-client who really wants to be on TV, he or she should consider professional media training.

LONG-TERM PR EFFORTS ARE KEY TO SUCCESS

Once the publicist has established the initial "buzz" for a new restaurant, the greatest challenge is maintaining publicity momentum over the long term. This is where the publicist must maximize his or her creative thinking. The main strategy is to design an ongoing series of special events aimed at most restaurants' primary sustaining audience—the immediate community in which they operate. Most of these events should involve local civic dignitaries who are key "opinion molders" or "centers of influence"—a basic communications campaign target in swaying public opinion in the surrounding community.

Of course there are some restaurants, especially in high-profile cities such as New York and Los Angeles, where publicists use the time-honored tactic of informing media columnists who was eating at the restaurant, and with whom. While this usually ends up in well-read social columns, such celebrity-sighting tactics can backfire. Not every celebrity wants their comings and goings to be fodder for the so-called gossip columnists. Some celebrities view such items as a privacy intrusion. This can mean they will never return to the restaurant, and may even tell their celebrity friends to avoid dining there unless they relish the paparazzi waiting to snap a candid photo. Nevertheless, if the goal is to create buzz, this is another way some publicists choose to beat the competition and extend the popularity of the dining spot.

CRITICAL REVIEWS

No matter what a PR person does to promote a restaurant, the one thing he or she cannot influence is the content of the much-anticipated review in local newspapers or influential food magazines. The "make or break" factor is strong when it comes to the power wielded by food reviewers. Their comments about the experience can apply across the board—everything from the décor and quality of food and service, to the lighting and menu design. While most reviewers visit several times and are anonymous, the smart publicist knows who the reviewers are and even what they look like. If the publicist has a relationship with the reviewer, based upon respect, even the most critical writer will sometimes give the restaurant several chances to redeem itself and earn a better review, if warranted. The bottom line is this: If the food is bad, the prices too high, and the service sub-par, not even a relationship will override a negative write-up.

Some publicists have mounted successful campaigns to recover from a poor review, by urging their restaurant client to take the write-up as constructive criticism and make the necessary changes. Often a new chef is brought in, an experienced host is hired, and the second review—in larger markets, at least a year later—can achieve a full turnaround. (See Sidebar 3-2, "Communicating with a Food Reviewer.")

As important as reviewers are to the success of a restaurant, so too are ratings from guides including Frommer's, Fodor's, and Zagat. In the annals of restaurant PR, perhaps the most influential words come from the food critic at *The New York Times*. A three- or four-star rating can bring diners in from across the country and set a restaurant on the fast track for success. The Mobil and AAA ratings are also important. A four- or five-star Mobil rating can launch even the most obscure restaurant into prominence. These ratings are annual, and it is important for the restaurant to retain or even improve its scores.

The "Academy Awards" for chefs are the James Beard Awards, named after the late cookbook author and "Dean of American Cookery," who defined the standards for culinary excellence.

SIDEBAR 3-2
COMMUNICATING WITH A FOOD REVIEWER
BY THOMAS HEAD
EXECUTIVE WINE AND FOOD EDITOR
THE WASHINGTONIAN MAGAZINE

In the world of food journalism, public relations gets a bad name, not from the people who do it well, but from the people who do it poorly. I'm the food editor and a restaurant reviewer for *The Washingtonian*, a city magazine that takes restaurants and food seriously. We know that food and dining out are subjects that our urban, sophisticated readership takes seriously.

Some PR people make my job a lot easier. They let me know about new restaurants and new trends. If I need information for a story, they're ready to brainstorm with me, even if it doesn't involve their own clients. They're fellow professionals.

Some PR people can be really annoying. They pitch stories that aren't appropriate for my magazine. They call after the fact demanding to know why they weren't mentioned in a particular story. They promise to send information that never appears.

The rules for dealing with restaurant reporters and reviewers aren't that different from the rules for dealing with any other kind of reporter, but I'll repeat a few of them and elaborate from my own point of view.

Know the publications you're pitching to. Writers get annoyed with PR people when they call up and try to pitch an idea that's just something the magazine would never do. I often want to say, "Why don't you take a look at this magazine then call me again?" It happens most often with agencies that have national accounts, but a surprising number of locals don't seem to have taken the trouble to read the publication.

My own magazine is extremely unlikely to do a feature story about a restaurant or chef until that person or restaurant has distinguished itself over time. We might do a review or a news item or mention the chef or restaurant in a roundup, but it's a waste of everybody's time to pitch the sort of story the magazine doesn't print.

Know the job of the person you're pitching a story or an event to. There are two different kinds of food writers—reporters and reviewers. A reviewer, whose reputation depends on being fair, tries to be as anonymous as possible. He or she is not likely to accept an invitation to dinner with a chef or PR person, and will not generally attend an opening party for a restaurant. Reviewers do, however, appreciate receiving invitations as a way of keeping up with what's going on. A person who reports on the restaurant scene rather than reviews restaurants is more likely to be able to accept a meal or an invitation to a party.

Pay attention to the magazine's publishing schedule. The Washingtonian works on a fairly tight schedule, and we can accept material until about six weeks in advance of the date of the issue. If you're sending me news for the October issue, I need it in the middle of August.

Don't tell me that you've bought advertising in the magazine. At our magazine, editorial and advertising are completely separate. I never get pressure to mention a restaurant or review it favorably because they're advertisers. Telling me that you've advertised is an insult to my editorial independence.

Be thorough. Send me a copy of the menu. Include a biography of the chef. Tell me what the place looks like. Write a cover letter telling me why I should care about the restaurant. You're much more likely to influence a review by telling me about the chef's background and training than by praising his cooking. Pay particular attention to the facts. I've received press releases that don't include the address or phone number of the restaurant.

Go easy on the adjectives. I don't need a press release to tell me that something is "delicious" or "unique." I'll taste it and decide that for myself.

Proofread. Editors and reporters are in the word business and are almost sure to notice mistakes in grammar, usage, or spelling. If these are areas where you're weak, have someone else proofread your work for you. This is particularly important if your menu contains foreign words or phrases. Don't assume that people won't notice—mistakes create an impression of amateurishness and sloppiness. It's "vinaigrette," not "vinegarette." Make absolutely sure your facts are correct—names, addresses, hours of operation, phone numbers. Messages correcting mistakes tend to get lost.

Return phone calls promptly. Reporters usually have questions when they're writing, and when they're writing, they're usually up against a deadline. If a reporter needs to know something that he or she can't find out, the story is in jeopardy.

Remember that PR is a long-range activity. It's often hard to convince clients, who want a big splash of publicity for an opening or an event, of this fact. But the most successful restaurant and hotel PR people are people who are in their job for the long term and know that successful PR depends on cultivating a network of acquaintances and building their confidence over time.

Think of ways to keep your clients on reporters' radar screens. If I'm doing a piece on restaurants that are serving bison or ostrich or organic beef, I'm much more likely to think of a place that has sent me a menu or a letter last week than one that sent a single press release for its opening. The best PR people think of ways to tie what their clients are doing to events that are likely to be on a magazine's editorial calendar—a presidential election or inauguration, outdoor dining in summer, hot toddies in winter. Savvy restaurant owners know that PR doesn't end with the opening party.

Remember that a bad review is better than no review. Avoid burning bridges. I get three kinds of responses to unfavorable reviews:

1. None, which is fine.

2. "Thank you for the review. We're looking into how to correct the unfavorable things you mentioned." That's probably unnecessary, but it's fine too.

3. "How dare you say these things about my restaurant. You're never welcome to come here again." I never will.

Restaurant PR people can arrange for their chefs to cook at the James Beard House in New York City if the chef shows true talent. A successful dinner can start "foodies," or food lovers, talking, and a Beard Foundation nomination for a chef in one of several award categories can sometimes follow.

TYPICAL MESSAGES AND MEDIA TARGETS

Typical PR messages or news hooks for restaurants include the following: the employment of new, highly-trained chefs; unique menu items; seasonal menu changes; facility improvements; anniversaries; and special events involving cooking classes, exclusive chef's tables, and meals inspired by motion pictures or general news coverage.

Publicity, which focuses on media placements, is the basic form of PR support that most restaurants seek. Among the key targets of monthly consumer publications are *Bon Appetit* (circ.: 1.3 million); *Gourmet* (circ.: 975,216); *Food and Wine* (circ.: 943,710), and the semimonthly *Wine Spectator* (circ.: 323,605). Celebrity chefs such as Emeril Lagasse and Wolfgang Puck attract huge TV audiences on networks such as The Food Channel and on morning programs such as NBC's *Today;* ABC's *Good Morning, America;* and CBS's *Early Show.*

PR practitioners who can arrange for their restaurant chefs to appear with the celebrity cooks can reap great benefits for their chef's reputation and the success of the restaurant. Destination travel writers often include coverage of restaurants and chefs in their stories about visiting cities and countries. Celebrity cooks appearing on-site can also be a big attraction.

Another important PR strategy is the publication of a cookbook. When chefs write a cookbook, it is usually to both enhance their own reputation and that of their restaurant. It is often up to the PR person to help launch the publicity campaign for the book, generate interviews for the chef, and keep the name of the cookbook on the radar screen for serious "foodies." Also, cookbook signings by famous chefs can be a big draw.

Not all restaurant publicity is without emergency challenges. An effective restaurant publicist occasionally must deal with a variety of crises. These can include the following: the departure of a well-established local chef; food poisoning incidents; poor health department ratings; accusations of discriminatory hiring and serving practices; and downgraded guide ratings. A true PR professional knows these things can happen and has a crisis communication plan ready for implementation at the first hint of a crisis.

Communicating in the Language of Food and Beverage

Culinary jargon can be intimidating even for the most seasoned practitioner. For the novice it can be absolutely daunting. That is why experts in the field recommend that PR newcomers engage in a serious self-study program to quickly learn some of the basic esoteric terminology common to the food and beverage business. This is imperative not only for precise conversations with chefs, kitchen staff, and sommeliers, but also for knowledgeable pitching and entertaining of food writers.

The experts' recipe for a "crash course" in learning the language of food and wine consists of heavy doses of reading of available literature—including the high-circulation consumer publications mentioned earlier, plus trade publications such as *Restaurants and*

Institutions, Art Culinaire, Food Arts, Nation's Restaurant News, Chocolatier, and *Pastry Arts and Design*.

In addition, the experts recommend these basic reference books: *The Chef's Companion: A Dictionary of Culinary Terms,* by Elizabeth Riley; *The Ethnic Food Lover's Companion,* by Eve Zibart; and *The New Food Lover's Companion: Comprehensive Definitions of Nearly 6,000 Food, Drink and Culinary Terms* (Baron's Cooking Guide), by Sharon Tyler Herbst.

Transportation Public Relations

Transportation is one of the most expansive sectors of travel and tourism PR because of its multiplicity of components. Among them are passenger railroads such as Amtrak, rental car companies, recreation vehicles, and motor coach companies. But the two most dominant components at this time are the airlines and the cruise ship lines. Since the start of the new millennium the former—particularly the long-established carriers—have been severely battered by the effects of new terrorism threats and other factors, while cruise ship lines have become one of the fastest-growing travel and tourism transportation modes. Airline and cruise ship PR are therefore the two selected focal points of this chapter.

AIRLINE PR

Airlines were the principal transportation mode for the 40.4 million foreign travelers to the United States in 2003. And that same year, airlines accounted for 16 percent of the total domestic U.S. person-trips. Despite this dominance and the record number of air travelers at the beginning of the new millennium, the airline industry was hard hit by the deadly terrorism attacks against the United States on Sept. 11, 2001. By 2004, passenger traffic had returned to the pre-9/11 levels, but airline revenues did not similarly rebound in the interim, owing to the onset of several new factors.

The adverse impact on air travel caused by 9/11, plus the advent of many new low-fare carriers in the new millennium, such as Southwest Airlines, JetBlue, and Air Tran, jeopardized the financial future of the so-called "legacy carriers"—the long-established lines that include American, United, Delta, US Airways, Northwest, and Continental. Other factors negatively impacting the revenues of the legacy carriers were the Iraq war, the Severe Acute Respiratory Syndrome (SARS) epidemic in 2003, and rising oil prices.

At press time for this book, labor unrest, falling revenues, and bankruptcies involving most of the legacy carriers had left their continued survival in question; a reshaping of the future infrastructure of the entire airline industry is possible.

Of all the travel and tourism sectors, the practice of PR in the airline industry is perhaps the most far-reaching. For example, airline headquarters PR staffs are among the largest, they use a wide range of PR tools, they target a vast number of media outlets and audiences, they communicate a greater variety of messages, and their crisis communication plans are some of the most comprehensive and sophisticated.

Internal PR Staffing and Organization

Typical legacy carrier headquarters PR department staff functions are aligned with their primary audiences. The size of media relations staffs can vary from three to ten, depending on the size of the company, mainly because of the inordinate number of daily press inquiries (one major airline reported a range of 30–40 inquiries on a normal day, versus 80–90 if a particular issue is raging that day). When they are not "putting out fires" these staffers are engaged in normal publicity activities and crisis planning, implementing special promotional campaigns, organizing special events and press trips, or assisting other department functions. The larger media relations staffs are further justified because this function operates both around the clock and around the world, as does today's news media. (See Sidebar 4-1, "Airline Media Relations: Buckle Up for 'Round-the-Clock Turbulence.")

A second major function usually supported by a staff of two or more is employee relations. The employee audience is a high priority for the following reasons: (1) Airlines consider their employees front-line PR representatives with the traveling public, and everyone needs to be "on the same page" in terms of disseminating consistent airline information; and (2) because up to 75 percent of legacy airline employees are union members it is imperative to keep them apprised of all company developments in order to earn their support for new policies and changes.

If the PR department is responsible for government affairs, there may be as many as five staffers assigned to the function—two for liaison with federal regulatory agencies and Congress, two for coordination with state and local government agencies, and an administrative coordinator.

If the PR department is fully responsible for consumer affairs, this could add as many as 70 or more individuals to the PR department staff. However, this function more often than not is located in other corporate departments such as marketing or corporate

SIDEBAR 4-1
AIRLINE MEDIA RELATIONS: BUCKLE UP FOR 'ROUND-THE-CLOCK TURBULENCE
BY CHRIS BARNETT
AIRLINES, BUSINESS TRAVEL, AND PR WRITER; CO-FOUNDER AND SENIOR EDITOR, *BULLDOG REPORTER*

Virtually no other industry in American business is under the media microscope more than commercial air travel. Almost daily, there is an airline-related story in the international, national, or community press. With the exception of "necessity of life stories" that impact our daily lives, such as health care, only the airlines—"steel birds" or the "tin" as they are known among airplane buffs—get more ink, air time and, now, cyber coverage.

Air travel and airlines today is a news beat, not just a mode of transportation. And with worldwide news organizations feeding a 24-hour news cycle, the media relations professional must have a global perspective plus the energy, agility, and communications skills to serve deadline-driven journalists—all of whom think they are your only priority.

Airline media relations is, flat out, the toughest, most demanding PR job in the travel and hospitality industry today. Air travel has been morphing for the last five decades from class to mass and, since 2000, it has been changing at warp speed.

After 2000, the mainstays of the U.S. airline industry were hammered by a seemingly endless stream of convulsive shocks: the Internet-fueled bubble burst; the U.S. stock market melted down, after which business travelers stayed in their offices; the terrorist attacks of 9/11 triggered the Iraq war and kept leisure travelers at home; jet fuel prices soared; airlines went bankrupt or teetered on the brink; several airline CEOs were caught enriching themselves and their cronies while cutting frills and bleeding or firing their employees; and more air travelers switched to new low-cost carriers and brought their own food aboard. Meanwhile, the seismic shocks in the U.S. airline industry radiated to global carriers as well.

Airline Media Relations: From Glad-Handers to Press Strategists

Ironically—at a time when airlines and air travel became a daily beat for business journalists, not just travel editors, and the airline PR professional was becoming an endangered species—the camaraderie that had long existed between members of the press and airline PR people was deteriorating. It was a good thing because the airline media relations professional had co-opted business and travel journalists in the 1970s and 1980s. With the rare exception of a tragedy such as a crash, airline PR was mostly responding to media inquires on new routes and new aircraft, issuing press releases, and hosting the press at splashy events and inaugural trips. There was virtually no strategic outreach to creatively market air travel to new audiences other than through frequent flyer programs. Growing demand and brief air fare sales and discounts kept seats full—until, that is, 9/11, when virtually all of the old-line U.S. air carriers retrenched, pruned their media relations staffs, adopted a siege mentality with a newly invigorated, investigative press, while trying to stay airborne financially.

As this is written in early 2005, airline media relations is practiced in two dramatically different styles: proactive and reluctantly reactive. Among U.S. commercial airlines, only four are reaching out to communicate messages, clarify misconceptions, explain complex financial transactions and, in general, trying to distinguish themselves from their competition. The four are American, JetBlue, Southwest, and America West.

Of all the U.S. airlines, American has gone from a "what's-the-question, I'll-get-back-to-you" mind-set, to a concerted effort in making sure the press gets—and understands—the airline's various messages. To bolster its own staff efforts, American uses the services of a large PR agency with responsive publicists who will promptly track down answers for reporters on deadline. In addition, American has assigned two senior communications specialists from outside the airline industry to develop relationships with beat reporters on an individual basis.

The Tools You Need to Succeed

Do not even think of pursuing a career in airline media relations today without having a deep understanding of the commercial airline industry, its problems and opportunities, its history, its likely future, and its communications and marketing challenges. A candidate looking for on-the-job training today will never make it to the interview stage. You do not need a stack of press clippings on stories you've written and published on air travel—although it would certainly help you stand out from a pile of résumés. However, you must be able to demonstrate a real understanding of the rapidly evolving airline business and have well thought out solutions you can offer a prospective employer.

This advice is true whether you join the staff of a PR consultancy with an airline account or the media relations staff of the carrier itself. You must immerse yourself in the financial, marketing, regulatory, and customer service aspects of both the passenger and the cargo departments of an airline. Your personal research and reading of everything from *Wall Street Journal* and *New York Times* press coverage, to Wall Street industry analyst reports, to all of the relevant airline trade publications, will best prepare you for an interview.

EFFECTIVE MEDIA RELATIONS START WITH THE CEO

The heart of an airline media relations program is something you cannot control. The airlines with the best public perception and, most recently, the best profit performance, also have chief executive officers who can emotionally connect with their employees, the traveling public, and the press. Sounds quite trite but the airline industry is a "people business." It's not just transportation like trucking, railroads, and shipping. The single best asset an airline media relations practitioner can have is a CEO who is congenial, personable, and a brilliant, visionary airline operator. Three good examples: Herb Kelleher, founder-chairman of Southwest Airlines; Richard Branson, founder-CEO of Virgin-Atlantic Airways; and David Neeleman, CEO of JetBlue Airways.

Effective airline PR begins at the top with the CEO. If you have an airline top executive who can, in fact, make the all important emotional connection even if he or she is not all that charismatic, that person should meet the beat reporters—general news and trade press—to start building personal relationships. This is the single smartest contribution you can make to improving the airline's reputation and perception and in creating a good working relationship with the press that cover you and the industry. Face to face with reporters—either one at a time or in a small group—is crucial. Why? Because it is only human nature that the majority of the media, not all reporters and editors, tend to subliminally give the brand a break on negative coverage if they have that relationship established beforehand.

Conversely, the aloof, inaccessible CEO who has never met the media covering the brand, the company, or the industry, has no "goodwill" to call on in tough times. The top executive of any industry who hides behind a press spokesperson, does not take interviews out of fear or arrogance, and who issues terse "official statements" is perceived by the media as either arrogant, uncaring, incompetent, or "guilty as charged." The unprecedented rash of corporate scandals has made companies and CEOs who are not forthcoming suspect in the eyes of the media and in the court of public opinion.

BUILD YOUR REPUTATION AS A "PRO"

While you are working as a communicator for a particular airline, reporters are going to hold you accountable for either shoddy, "bush-league" media relations, or hold you in high esteem as helpful, smart, and knowledgeable. Building your own reputation is critical because reporters will go to PR people who "get it" instead of their counterparts who are slow to respond, have an "attitude" or, worse yet, don't, or cannot, get answers to the media questions.

One way to become valuable to the media is to identify for a reporter a corporate executive who can address the particular issue—and be a primary source for the media. In recent years, there has been a trend for the PR pro to be a "spokesperson" on an issue for the company. I consider this a lazy and dangerous response to media queries. There is virtually no way for the PR person to have the intimate, up-to-the-second intelligence that a line executive would have. Hence, he or she is simply transmitting information. Plus, that is usually in the form of a homogenized, soulless reply that has no color, feeling, or passion. In most cases, a reporter will give it scant use—an official response and nothing more.

The ideal media person should have access to, and an understanding of, the issues so he or she can offer context as background to give the reporter a richer, full-dimensioned response, and do it without giving away proprietary, corporate information that can compromise the company or divulge material financial information to one reporter that would lead to possible repercussions with regulatory agencies.

Of course, if you have a 9-to-5 mentality, you should cross airline media relations off your career list. You may work regular hours but you and your colleagues are "on duty" around-the-clock, seven days a week. Any emergency involving an airline is news because the public is involved, particularly if it's weather-related and hundreds or thousands of people are stranded. At these times, TV camera crews are swarming the airports seeking human interest comments that usually involve bashing the airline if it is not comforting the passengers and getting them on their way. The bigger the problem, naturally, the bigger the news.

Most airline media relations staffs rotate "press duty officer" responsibilities just like a doctor who is "on call" on weekends so colleagues can take time off. Airlines use the same strategy. But when a major problem occurs or tragedy strikes, you will be there to execute the airline's crisis communications strategy. Here is where a pro-active relationship with the news media pays off. One final piece of advice: keep the press advised on the facts you know—do not speculate—and keep them updated regularly.

By building a relationship with the media based on your ability to perform under pressure and provide forthright information with a minimum of spin, you are investing in your career. The press is fluid. Its members are mobile and move to other positions or other news outlets.

If you do your job The Right Way, you will have a leg up as a source to successor journalists, and you will be referred to other media covering the airline industry as a "sharp PR person who can make it happen."

If you earn that accolade early in your career, you have a bright future in airline media relations.

affairs. The airlines have traditionally put a high value on the consumer affairs function, which handles customer complaints, executive correspondence, and government compliance reports on travelers with disabilities, etc. In some instances, the consumer affairs division also is responsible for community relations activities if it operates in the PR department.

Since most U.S. airline companies are publicly traded, it is not uncommon for many airline PR departments to include one or two staffers to handle the investor relations function, which is charged with communicating with special financial audiences such as shareholders, financial analysts, and institutional investors. Some of the special PR tools used for these audiences include issuance of the annual report, quarterly earnings and dividend reports and news releases, and the organization of analyst presentations.

The staff number ranges cited in the typical airline PR department organization outline above are most applicable to the legacy carriers. Presently, the new low-fare carriers have much smaller internal PR staffs. But as they evolve, experts expect that their staff numbers and organization will more closely resemble those of the legacy carriers.

EXTENSIVE COMMUNICATIONS WITH EMPLOYEES AND CUSTOMERS

Airlines use nearly all of the available PR tools to communicate to their key audiences. A prime example is the employee public. Typical tools that airlines use to convey their messages to this important audience include daily electronic newslines, weekly or biweekly employee newsletters, intranet daily updates, daily distribution of news clipping packets, weekly recorded messages from the CEO, weekly calls with managers in the field to respond to rumors or to share themed "messages of the week," and quarterly meetings with senior officers to rotate through major employee locales. In addition, daily news and special updates are recorded so that employees who are traveling can phone in for company news. Also in wide use are Internet chat boards and webcasts.

A key airline medium for communicating with customers is the monthly "in-flight magazine." All of the legacy carriers distribute these magazines to passengers via placement in the pocket in back of each airplane seat. For example, the US Airways magazine, *Attache,* which has a circulation of 338,349, is "editorially targeted to the frequent business traveler," says *Bacon's Annual Magazine Directory.* "Features explore intriguing people and places throughout the country, with an accent on food and wine, the arts, recreational sports, historic and/or natural sites, and an insider's guide to American cities. Special sections offer readers perspectives on business and technology, as well as puzzles."

Each in-flight magazine also features a personal message to passengers from the CEO and destination articles that often reflect locales along the routes flown by the airline. These magazines are printed by outside specialty publication contractors, and many of the articles are written by established freelance travel writers.

As a primary transportation mode, the airlines are in the unique position of serving as a basic link between the other major travel and tourism sectors. This results in a tight interface with most of the same key audiences as the other sectors. This holds true especially for destinations and hotels, and their convention and visitor bureaus' (CVBs) allies. For example, it is common practice for these entities to team up in the sponsorship of mutually beneficial press tours.

One notable audience exception is travel agents, to whom airlines no longer pay commissions because of the need to eliminate high distribution costs. As more customers reserve their travel online, many travel agents have either ceased selling airline tickets or have begun charging customers a fee.

MULTILAYERED MEDIA TARGETS

The airlines' linkage with other travel and tourism sectors also means that airline media targets are multilayered. The airline business also cuts across a broader swath of media interests than do the other sectors. For example, environmental media are most interested in noise/pollution issues associated with flying. Wine and food writers often show an interest in airline food offerings. And the consumer advocacy media are very interested in airline accommodations for physically disabled flyers.

Like their sector counterparts, the airlines have their own share of trade publications to address. These include *Aviation Week & Space Technology,* with a circulation of over 100,000; *Aviation Daily; Airways;* and *Air Transport World.* Industry-related trade publications that airline spokespeople must also deal with are those covering pilots, airports, outer space, flying safety, and aeronautics.

But because of the financial turbulence besetting the legacy carriers the past decade, the airline media segment that has preoccupied many practitioners has been the financial/business press. As a result, airline spokespeople, in sharp contrast with their industry counterpart sectors, have been forced to operate on an almost daily crisis footing. This is a most unfortunate circumstance because it puts airline PR staffs in a constant reactive mode that hinders pro-active efforts to effectively promote many positive initiatives such as the inauguration of new services, special fare promotions, and community outreach activities.

When it comes to managing crises, however, the airlines are far from neophytes. In fact, they are among the nation's leaders in the efficient handling of disaster situations, and their emergency plans have often been held up as models for other companies in terms of prearranged duty assignments, recall procedures, employment of emergency Web sites, support for affected families, and government/community liaison.

When a plane accident occurs, the involved airline functions as a primary source of information for the media. Up until the National Transportation Safety Board (NTSB) takes control of the accident scene (normally within four to six hours), the airline PR staff is responsible for disseminating facts about the aircraft, its passengers, and the crew.

During that window, the airline CEO normally rushes to the scene, meets with the press, and issues a statement, offering condolences, and citing his carriers' safety record. After the NTSB takes over, airline PR staffers assume day-to-day duties for responding to media follow-up questions.

While there have been a number of high-profile plane crashes over the years, industry professional organizations such as the Air Transport Association are quick to point out that, historically, flying remains the safest mode of transportation.

CRUISE LINE PR

For many years, cruise ships were often referred to as "floating hotels." Today, the more apt nickname would be "floating hotels, restaurants, and resorts" because of the multiple new guest services being offered as a total package.

These changes closely resemble those now being offered by the upscale segment of the hotel industry. As a result, the communication components of cruise line PR are very similar to those of hotels. For example, they have similar messages to the media; similar key audiences, such as guests, travel writers, and travel agents; similar PR tools, such as press kits, Web sites, and B-roll; and similar media targets, such as hotel, restaurant, and travel consumer and trade publications.

CRUISE INDUSTRY PROFESSIONAL ASSOCIATIONS

Leading the cruise industry's PR and marketing efforts is the Cruise Lines International Association (CLIA), which is based in New York City and represents 95 percent of cruise capacity from North America. The membership includes 19 of the major lines serving North America and nearly 17,000 travel agency members. CLIA conducts various training and certification programs to assist agents in selling cruise business.

Among CLIA's major member lines are Carnival Cruise Lines, Celebrity Cruises, Costa Cruises, Crystal Cruises, Cunard Line, Disney Cruise Line, Holland American Line, Norwegian Cruise Lines, Orient Lines, Princess Cruise, Royal Caribbean International, Seabourn Cruiseline, Silversea Cruises, and Windstar Cruises.

The industry's chief advocate in the U.S. capital is the International Council of Cruise Lines (ICCL). It participates in regulatory and policy development, and promotes safe, secure, and healthy cruise environments.

SOARING INDUSTRY GROWTH BENEFITS U.S. ECONOMY

Cruise lines have been a steady star performer in the transportation sector of travel and tourism over the past several decades. In 1980, just over one million passengers traveled aboard cruise ships. Since then, that number has grown at an average annual rate of 8.1 percent, to nearly 10 million in 2004, according to CLIA.

Approximately 20 North American cruise lines today operate a total of 184 ships, generating a total U.S. economic impact of $25.4 billion and more than 295,000 jobs, according to a recent ICCL study. From 2000 to 2005, a major building boom was capped by 62 new ships in the North American market.

Prior to the modern era of growth for cruise lines (1980 to the present), the industry was struggling to survive. The industry had a stodgy, formal, and elitist reputation. Factors boosting the industry's impressive resurgence included expansion of the fleet, the decentralizing of "homeporting" beyond the Miami area to ports on the other U.S. seacoasts, and the introduction of a host of service innovations that strongly appealed to the aging and affluent "baby boomer" generation.

Multiple New Cruise Line Experiences

Among the innovations that have helped to update the cruise line image are increased shipboard activities, a greater number of excursions, a more casual ambiance, and extensive children's programs. These new services, supported by some highly effective PR campaigns, have transformed the entire industry and replaced its staid image with a much more contemporary look.

As a result, most of the present PR messages communicated today to potential customers are focused on the vast variety of experiences now available on many cruise line sailings. These experiences coincide with these specific examples of new ship services and features: relaxed dress requirements; room service and multiple restaurants offering a variety of cuisines, in place of a single main dining room; numerous children's activities including in-line skating, skateboarding, and rock-climbing walls; expanded adult venues including casinos, technology centers, aerobics exercise rooms, spas, and various "enrichment programs" featuring cultural/educational/health/investment lectures and demonstrations; and more diverse shoreside excursions that capitalize on trendy new niche tourism interests such as adventure tourism, eco-tourism, and cultural tourism.

Similarities to the Practice at Hotels

Like hotels, extensive communications with guests is a top priority for cruise line PR practitioners. Comprehensive and often glossy pre-cruise information kits are furnished to prospective guests. During cruises, guests receive daily printed newsletters in their suites that profile interesting crew members, preview upcoming excursions and destinations, and highlight daily restaurant menus and entertainment. Guests also are sometimes given access to daily international news summaries. Similar to repeat business incentive programs in the hotel and airline industries, cruise lines offer their best customers special values and discounts through various customer loyalty programs that are touted through collateral material distributed during voyages.

One of the most effective PR tools for the industry are familiarization ("fam") tours for travel writers and travel agents. In fact, it is not unusual for the cruise lines to sometimes collaborate with hotels at relevant ports of call in the sponsorship of these influential groups. Cruise lines also make extensive use of B-roll for broadcast media outlets and videotapes for travel agency use. Web sites, too, are a primary information source for both customers and the media. And special events are commonplace for drawing attention to newly launched ships and maiden voyages, and new ports of call, itineraries, and services. (See Sidebar 4-2, "Launching Queen Mary 2: A Public Relations Case Study.")

CRUISE LINE MEDIA, PR STAFFING, AND CRISIS PLANNING

Among the leading industry trade media are *Cruise Week, Cruise Industry News,* and *Cruise News Daily.* Leading industry consumer media include the bimonthly *Cruise Travel* (circ. 153,645) and *Porthole Cruise Magazine.* Other key media targets include *Travel Weekly* and *Travel Agent*—which run regular sections covering industry news—and *The New York Times, The Los Angeles Times, The Washington Post, The Miami Herald,* and *The San Francisco Chronicle*—which periodically print cruise feature sections.

From a PR staffing perspective, cruise line PR staffing is relatively small compared to most hotel chains. Full-time practitioners are based mostly at the corporate headquarters. But large-scale use is made of outside PR agencies/counsel for special events. In general, PR-related activities aboard the ships on routine voyages are accomplished by designated crew members such as the cruise director or guest services personnel.

Cruise lines certainly are not immune to emergencies, although the incident rate in recent years has been low. Evacuation drills today are a standard procedure aboard ships. Among the scenarios for which most lines have developed crisis communications plans are onboard fires, sinkings, collisions, viral outbreaks, pollution incidents, and terrorist attacks. The latter scenario became a reality in October 1985 when the Italian cruise ship *Achille Lauro* was hijacked in the Mediterranean Sea by Palestinian terrorists; the hijackers killed a disabled American passenger named Leon

SIDEBAR 4-2
LAUNCHING *QUEEN MARY 2:* A PUBLIC
RELATIONS CASE STUDY
BY VIRGINIA M. SHERIDAN, PRESIDENT
M. SILVER ASSOCIATES, INC.
NEW YORK, N.Y.

Cunard Line's *Queen Mary 2*, the $800-million luxury ocean liner, made her inaugural voyage in January 2004. Within weeks of her arrival in North America, the ship's entire 2004 schedule was sold out. Eighteen months before the first sailing some $50 million in reservations had been accepted. More than 60 percent of bookings represented new customers for the venerable cruise company. In an agreement destined to generate even more invaluable worldwide attention, *QM2* was named the flagship of the 2004 Olympic Games in Athens, Greece.

Does marketing deserve all the credit for this impressive success? Of course not: when the world's tallest, widest, fastest, and most expensive cruise ship is introduced, the product generates considerable interest all on its own. Nevertheless, the two-year public relations campaign created and implemented for Cunard by M. Silver Associates, a New York-based agency specializing in travel and tourism, was an extraordinary success with measurable results, a success that resulted in the "*QM2* Effect"—a significant boost in cruise sales across the industry that even Cunard's rivals attribute to the attention generated by *QM2*. It even overcame obstacles that advertising and sales could not address.

The story of *Queen Mary 2* begins with a bold decision to build the defining ocean liner for the 21st century. The ultimate success of this ambitious venture rested on answering this question: Is *QM2* the cruise vacation product for today's affluent, discriminating traveler? Cunard Line officials clearly thought so. For M. Silver Associates, the challenge was to convince the traveling public that Cunard was right.

A Historical Perspective

To an industry that is remarkably young, Cunard Line brings a unique historical perspective as well as a dynamic vision of the future. Both are perfectly represented in the launch of *Queen Mary 2.*

The birth of today's booming cruise industry was foretold by a milestone event in the history of transportation: in 1959, for the first time, more people traveled by air across the Atlantic Ocean than by ship. The writing was on the wall: if the public preferred to *travel* quickly, then the purpose of ocean-going ships would have to be redefined or they risked quick obsolescence. That new purpose was to be the concept of *vacationing* by ship.

Initially built upon a fleet of former ocean liners suddenly left with few passengers to transport, the cruise industry—pioneered with three older ships by Carnival Cruise Lines—has been transformed completely in the last 30 years. In the last 15 years alone, more than 125 new cruise vessels went into service.

Cunard Line's role in this success story has been and continues to be unique. Cunard was the first company to offer regularly scheduled transatlantic service beginning in the 1840s. For most of the 20th century, the company set the standard for elegant shipboard travel as reflected in messages such as

"The Only Way to Cross" that became icons of advertising. For captains of industry, heads of state and major political figures, celebrities, and famous sports figures, the grand ocean liners of Cunard became synonymous with the finest things in life. It is remarkable that its success today is, in large part, based on offering a 21st century version of the very travel experience that doomed the other shipping companies: a regular schedule of transatlantic sailings.

A NEW QUEEN FOR A NEW CENTURY'S EXPECTATIONS

The success of *Queen Mary 2* depends on meeting and even exceeding the expectations of today's affluent yet value-conscious travelers, many of whom represent demographics not traditionally associated with luxury cruising. While the wealthy retirees continue to be a significant factor, so too are baby boomers who may have never considered a cruise before as well as physically active vacationers, and travelers seeking intellectual and spiritual stimulation. Many of these potential Cunard cruisers had new attitudes about where and how they receive information and advice, and what or who they trust in making travel decisions.

In reaching this broad spectrum of customers, M. Silver Associates had the ideal product to work with. Cunard's ship for the 21st century was nothing short of revolutionary. Its physical design celebrated luxury ocean liner tradition and history while incorporating the most modern expectations of comfort and technology features. Oxford University provided a comprehensive program of onboard learning. The Royal Academy of Dramatic Art of London was a key feature of a multifaceted entertainment program. The dining experience ranged from celebrity chef Todd English's own restaurant and Cunard's exclusive, signature Princess and Queens Grills, to Kings Court, a collection of four boutique restaurants including a Chef's Galley where guests learn to cook from experts, to the grand, three-story Britannia Restaurant. Canyon Ranch, the North American leader in spas, fitness centers, and beauty facilities, operated the spa.

Luxury amenities were addressed with such features as the Veuve Clicquot Champagne Bar and an Hermès boutique at sea as well as accommodations—ranging from cabins to super-luxury duplex apartments with private butlers—with private labeled Simmons mattresses covered by Frette linens. Waterford Wedgwood provided porcelain and crystal for dining rooms, bars, and the champagne bar. And throughout, every aspect of the shipboard experience was informed by the superb standard of Cunard White Star service.

The Challenges

Despite having an outstanding and truly unique product to market, M. Silver Associates (MSA) had a number of challenges to overcome. *Queen Mary 2* was being launched at a time when the United States and many other national economies were tenuous at best and large numbers of affluent consumers had been hard hit by stock market declines in the past few years. The cruise industry itself continued to be buffeted by intense price competition driven by oversupply and weak demand, again due to the economy. Despite Cunard's virtual monopoly of regularly scheduled transatlantic service, the demand for this cruise experience had a very small margin of error; one too many voyages or one too few could mean the difference between profit and loss.

In addition, the Cunard brand itself was at a turning point. After undergoing numerous changes of ownership and management, and downsizing of product over the last decade or so—with sometimes dramatic reverses in direction with each one—Cunard's image in the marketplace was fuzzy at best and, in some important respects, outdated and tired. The line's flagship, *Queen Elizabeth 2,* though an iconic figure in the industry, was approaching 40 years old and newer ships had stolen her thunder.

Against this backdrop, MSA was asked to create brand distinction for Cunard Line in large part by making its past become the future in the minds of consumers and the travel trade. At the same time, the agency needed to make ocean travel (as opposed to "every day another port" cruising) immensely appealing. And to further distinguish the brand from other cruise lines, there was a need to communicate the "Britishness" of the *Queen Mary 2* and, by extension, Cunard Line itself.

THE CAMPAIGN

To accomplish these goals, M. Silver's task was to generate the highest possible levels of excitement, awareness, and demand for *QM2* prior to and during its inaugural voyage, with ongoing public relations activities afterward. The campaign was a mix of media relations, promotions, product and event tie-ins, and special events.

The strategy of the campaign was to capitalize on Cunard's 165 years of history and British heritage to create a new generation of transatlantic passengers and restore the company's luster and reputation, generate pre-launch "buzz" by highlighting the uniqueness of the ship's attributes, focus attention on Cunard's senior management and the uniqueness of having all women in senior positions, leverage key partnerships with well-known brands that would be featured on the ship, showcase the ship to key media, and secure high-profile celebrity events.

Pre-launch activities included the creation of a defining positioning statement for the ship—"the tallest, widest, longest and most expensive ocean liner ever built"—that was used in all communications vehicles; arranging interviews, press conferences, and broadcast appearances for Cunard management; and staging publicity-generating media events that included a dinner at *Bon Appetit* magazine with chef Todd English to debut his restaurant concept, a preview of *QM2* custom-designed Wedgwood/Waterford china and crystal at the British Ambassador's residence in New York, and a Canyon Ranch press luncheon with travel, beauty, and spa media.

Other pre-launch activities included shipyard visits for cruise journalists to see the ship "in the making"; announcing major construction milestone events with press releases, photography, and video news releases for national broadcast; a comprehensive press kit; a "Countdown to *QM2*" e-newsletter; and other communications devices.

For the launch itself, MSA secured top-rated national morning and entertainment television shows, including 15 minutes on *The Today Show*, three days on *Good Morning America*, and coverage on the *CBS Early Show*, as well as on the *Late Show with David Letterman, CNBC News* with Brian Williams, the *NBC Nightly News, MSNBC, CNN Daybreak*, a feature on *Live! With Regis and Kelly*, and an entire week on

Entertainment Tonight. MSA generated coverage in over 100 national and regional newspapers as well as most of the major travel and lifestyle magazines; hosted over 400 media on preview cruises to Southampton and the United States; and promoted gala christening ceremonies, sea trials, and ship arrivals in Fort Lauderdale, Brazil, and New York.

To celebrate the start of her transatlantic season and her first-ever arrival in New York City, the agency secured a major charity event—Katie Couric's star-studded fundraiser, the Entertainment Industry Foundation's second *Hollywood Hits Broadway* gala to benefit the National Colorectal Cancer Research Alliance—and managed her historic arrival with a live press conference with the mayor of New York and 150 media and her departure four days later with her sister ship, *Queen Elizabeth 2*—the first time that two Cunard "Queens" have sailed together in 60 years.

By any standards of measurement, M. Silver Associates' public relations campaign for *Queen Mary 2* ranks as a great success.

Klinghoffer and threw his body overboard. In the wake of increased worldwide terrorism threats, cruise lines have strengthened their security measures, including the use of passenger and baggage screening devices and closer identification checks. During the immediate post-9/11 period, the cruise lines were especially effective in adapting to the situation. For example, they began modifying itineraries to accommodate customers, and began using more homeports so passengers would not have to fly to get to their vacation.

PR at Other Selected Transportation Services

In addition to airline and cruise line PR efforts in the travel and tourism transportation sector, PR in the following components is especially noteworthy.

Automobile PR and the American Automobile Association (AAA)

In the United States, private automobile travel is the most popular form of transportation, according to the Travel Industry Association of America (TIA), accounting for 78 percent of all person-trips. And one of the most prominent organizations supporting American automobile travelers is the American Automobile Association (AAA), whose activities cut across all four of the major sectors of travel and tourism despite the national recognition it enjoys mainly for its excellent roadside service programs. Consider these points:

1. AAA's approximately 70 clubs across the nation collectively comprise the eighth largest travel agency in the United States.

2. AAA is the largest travel publisher in the world, printing more than 200 titles a year. Two of its bimonthly magazines,

AAA Going Places and *AAA World,* each of which boasts a circulation of over 2 million, rank as the largest consumer publications in the travel and tourism industry. Other organization publications include maps, TripTiks, and TourBook guides.

3. AAA is one of the travel industry's most prestigious hotel and restaurant rating services. Sixty-five full-time AAA evaluators annually rate 55,000 North American lodging and restaurant establishments using a system of diamonds to connote the quality of service and accommodations (five diamonds equals the highest grade).

The organization's PR staff consists of eight professionals—five at the national headquarters in Heathrow, Fla., and three more at the headquarters office in Washington, D.C. Most of the AAA clubs around the country assign an employee to perform PR duties on a part-time basis, but the largest usually have at least one permanent PR practitioner on staff.

Primary audiences for AAA PR are its 48 million members and its 38,000 employees. In addition to its many member publications and Web site, the AAA PR department regularly communicates with employees through targeted e-mails and a monthly magazine.

Much of the staff's time is devoted to media relations activities aimed at the driving public, and AAA spokespersons do frequent TV on-camera and live radio interviews to deliver messages on topics such as driving safety tips, gasoline pricing, and holiday traffic statistics.

One notable nationwide AAA public service program initiated by the organization's PR department is the AAA Travel High School Challenge, which awards $156,000 in student scholarships based on test results. The project is aimed at enhancing travel destination and geographic literacy.

Train Travel PR and Amtrak

Intercity passenger transportation by rail in the United States is primarily aboard Amtrak trains, and the passenger traffic is significant. In fiscal year 2004, 25 million passengers—an all-time record—rode Amtrak trains serving 500 stations in 46 states. Besides operating its own 22,000-mile rail system, Amtrak also supports intercity commuter rail services that transport 850,000 passengers each weekday. The Virginia Railway Express (VRE) and Maryland Area Regional Commuter (MARC) are examples of these commuter trains in the Washington, D.C., metropolitan area.

The organization is a quasi-government corporation dependent upon federal funding. Its PR support comes from a small in-house department of six professionals. A key department function is media relations, which entails interaction with national and local journalists who primarily focus on business/financial aspects of the corporation. Department media spokespersons operate out of the Washington, D.C., headquarters and hubs in Chicago and Oakland, Calif., and they are on-call 24 hours per day. The Amtrak PR department has earned a solid reputation for its crisis communications management in instances of occasional derailments, train collisions, and power outages.

Besides its active attention to its media audience, the Amtrak PR staff communicates with two other principal audiences: its millions of passengers and its thousands employees. Passengers receive Amtrak messages mainly through the company's consumer-driven Web site and Amtrak's monthly *Arrive Magazine,* which is aimed at riders of its busiest line along the Northeast Corridor. Employees are kept informed via a monthly tabloid newspaper, *Amtrak Inc.,* and targeted e-mails that are updated weekly.

Monthly magazine targets for Amtrak news are the trade publications *Railway Age* and *Progressive Railroading,* and the consumer publication *Trains*.

5

Destination and Tourist
Attraction PR

The term "destinations" in the context of this chapter refers to popular U.S. visitor sites such as the Hawaiian Islands, Florida's beaches, New York's Catskill Mountains, Arizona's Grand Canyon, California's Napa Valley, Nevada's casinos, Colorado's Rocky Mountains, the Washington, D.C. area's landmarks, and the National Park System. Tourist attractions including museums, historical monuments and sites, cultural centers and theme or amusement parks, and mega-shopping malls are all "travel destinations within travel destinations." These tourist attractions share many key audiences with destinations. Also, attractions and destinations often cooperatively promote their respective locales and attractions. This is why they are treated jointly in this chapter.

DOMESTIC TRAVELERS AND INTERNATIONAL VISITORS

The primary market for destinations and tourist attractions is leisure travel. This market is composed of both domestic and international travelers. In 2003, the Travel Industry Association of America (TIA) reported a total of 1.14 billion domestic U.S. person-trips. The top five state destinations that year were California, Florida, Texas, Pennsylvania, and New York. In 2000, total domestic and international traveler spending (in billions) in those states, respectively, was $78, $60, $36, $16, and $40.

Once U.S. travelers reach their destination, what activities are they most interested in? According to a 2003 TIA survey, shopping tops the list, followed by: attending a social or family event; outdoor activity; city/urban sightseeing; rural sightseeing; beaches; historic places/museums; gambling; theme/amusement parks; and visits to national or state parks. The top modes of transportation were automobile/truck/RV (78%) and airplane (16%).

In terms of international visitors, the United States (according to the World Tourism Organization) in 2003 ranked third in the world with 40.4 million, surpassed only by France (75 million) and Spain (52.5 million). However, the United States led the world in 2003 in total foreign tourist receipts with $65.1 billion. The main overseas regions from which this traffic originated were Europe, Asia, and South America.

PR for tourist attractions begins at the local level; is reinforced by town, city and regional convention and visitor bureaus (CVBs); and is further enhanced by the support received from U.S. state and territory tourism offices.

Top 10 U.S. City Destinations for Overseas Travelers in 2003 (in millions of arrivals)

City	Number of Arrivals
New York City	4.0 million
Los Angeles	2.2 million
Miami	2.2 million
Orlando	1.8 million
San Francisco	1.6 million
Honolulu	1.6 million
Las Vegas	1.2 million
Metro D.C. Area	901,000
Chicago	721,000
Boston	721,000

Source: U.S. Office of Travel and Tourism Industries, Department of Commerce.

Local attractions—such as natural scenic wonders, museums, historical sites, theme/amusement parks, national and state parks, recreational areas, cultural centers, and sporting venues—typically use these basic PR tools to promote their locations: color brochures, dedicated Web sites, B-roll, news releases, fact sheets, videos, and press kits. The smaller attractions usually employ area PR firms or counselors on a part-time basis to prepare these materials, while larger enterprises such as the major amusement parks frequently have sizable in-house PR staffs, supplemented by outside PR agency support.

CVBs AND STATE TOURISM OFFICES

Convention and visitor bureaus vastly expand the scope and reach of local attraction PR efforts. According to the Destination

Marketing Association International (DMAI), CVBs are not-for-profit organizations charged with representing a specific destination and helping with the long-term development of communities through a travel and tourism strategy. They usually are membership organizations bringing together businesses that rely on tourism and meetings for revenue.

For visitors, CVBs are like the "keys to the city." As an unbiased resource, CVBs can serve as broker or an official point of contact for convention and meeting planners, tour operators, and visitors. CVBs do not charge for services rendered because most are funded through a combination of hotel occupancy taxes and membership dues.

From a PR standpoint, CVBs function as a central clearinghouse of information about their destination for media around the world. For example, they maintain Web sites that highlight most local attractions and destinations; they publish consolidated local guidebooks, maps, and seasonal special event calendars; and they help arrange area itineraries for visiting travel writers, whom they often will escort. CVB PR staffs also serve as area press spokespersons, and represent their clients at national and international trade shows. (See Sidebar 5-1, "How GMCVB Used PR to Promote Miami as a Diverse Destination.")

Representing destinations, tourist attractions, and their CVBs on a statewide basis are their respective state tourism offices (commonly located in the state capitals)—and nearly every U.S. state and territory has one. A 2003 TIA survey of the tourism budgets of these offices showed that 46 U.S. states (excluding New York, which did not furnish data) had total budgeted promotional expenditures of $549.5 million, or $11.9 million on average per state. The leading state spenders were Hawaii, Illinois, Pennsylvania, Texas, and Florida.

SIDEBAR 5-1
HOW GMCVB USED PR TO PROMOTE MIAMI AS A DIVERSE DESTINATION
BY JEANNE SULLIVAN, ASSOC. VP, MEDIA RELATIONS
GREATER MIAMI CONVENTION & VISITORS BUREAU (GMCVB)
MIAMI, FLORIDA

Although Miami has been a socially diverse destination with a rich arts community for a couple of decades, its reputation as a leading U.S. center for arts and cultural diversity took several years of concentrated public relations efforts to develop.

In the late 1990s, focus groups told the Greater Miami Convention & Visitors Bureau (GMCVB) that its diversity—both cultural and product—gave Miami a competitive edge over other warm weather destinations. No other destination has Miami's unique combination of tropical climate and natural wonders, combined with a sophisticated metropolis. For example, one of Miami's top competitors for tourism, the Caribbean, has beautiful beaches but no critical mass of world-class arts and culture, nightlife, shopping, cutting edge cuisine, or cultural diversity.

For this reason, the GMCVB stepped up its efforts to emphasize its new brand, highlighting its cosmopolitan aspects, from its multicultural flavor to its thriving arts community. This was a key strategy in helping to give travelers reasons to come to Miami other than just to escape the winter cold. One of the GMCVB's first initiatives was to hire one of the first Cultural Tourism Directors in the country to create a unified vision and voice among local arts groups and share resources. Few other CVBs had a dedicated staff person whose sole role was to promote cultural tourism, and few do today.

The new Cultural Tourism Director, George Neary, ran the Miami Design Preservation League and was active in the arts community. He immediately began to form initiatives that would bring low-budget but respected arts and culture groups on the same marketing page, from a Winter Stages of the Sun theater program, to International Museum Day, to creating an all-inclusive Multicultural Guide distributed to travel and meeting professionals as well as media visiting Miami. A new Heritage Guide was also developed, detailing Miami's rich but often unknown history and diverse ethnic cultures. The Heritage Guide in 2004 became the textbook for a new GMCVB-led Tour Guide Certification program, designed to help ensure Miami tour guides were more knowledgeable and professional.

GMCVB's public relations team worked in tandem with Neary to provide updated media materials on Miami's rich arts and cultural mix, pitching stories to media on the phone or at media marketplaces and hosting them on familiarization tours during multicultural events such as the Black Film Festival, Miami/Bahamas Goombay Festival, and Calle Ocho festival. Although GMCVB's sales and limited advertising also supported these efforts very cost-effectively, including advertising co-ops with cultural groups and bringing cultural groups to trade shows, the public relations efforts by far were the most critical in raising awareness of Miami's diversity. The millions of dollars of publicity generated over the past few years, reinforcing Miami's competitive brand, has been priceless.

Our limited advertising and sales budget could never buy the buzz generated by targeted PR efforts. Consumers value broadcast and print editorial much more as a destination endorsement than paid advertising and sales programs.

One of the most important GMCVB initiatives that made national news was its efforts to promote to what is now the coveted gay and lesbian travel market. Miami's was the first CVB to proactively promote to this lucrative market, which is very wealthy and highly resistant to market changes. The GMCVB conducted the first gay and lesbian media tour with the city of Miami Beach, making headlines in *Time* for this controversial move. Upon Versace's death, which brought a social backlash on gay lifestyles, the GMCVB continued to emphasize to media that what attracted celebrities such as Versace to Miami was its acceptance of diverse cultures and lifestyles. It began to bring international and domestic gay media to major gay and lesbian events, such as Winter Party, Aqua Girl, White Party, and the Gay & Lesbian Film Festival. It worked with the city of Miami Beach to market at major gay and lesbian trade shows and host floats and receptions at key Gay Pride events in New York, Toronto, and Sao Paolo.

Another way in which GMCVB worked with its industry partners—such as the city of Miami Beach, the city of Miami, and Miami-Dade County—to reinforce its brand was to bring in one of the leading arts shows in the world to Miami. Art Basel, the premier gallery show in the world, based in Basel, Switzerland, was looking for a city to make its U.S. debut in the winter. The GMCVB and partners lobbied and won a three-year contract, which has proven enormously successful. GMCVB and local partners worked with Swiss organizers to make Art Basel Miami Beach even more popular than the original, providing world-class arts and entertainment venues for show events and exclusive after-parties. Record attendees come annually to enjoy the warm winter weather and the sophisticated internationally friendly arts infrastructure. GMCVB worked with Art Basel Miami Beach officials to bring in dozens of major international and domestic press to cover the glamour and cutting-edge art, as well as Miami's year-round hip arts and entertainment scene.

GMCVB's integrated marketing efforts, especially its cost-effective PR efforts, have garnered invaluable publicity that advertising can't buy. By consistently looking for opportunities over the past few years to reinforce Miami's brand as a hip cultural, cosmopolitan community in the global media, the GMCVB's PR team has helped make Miami a place people want to visit year-round—not just the winter. By promoting exciting arts, culture, and entertainment programs that are available for discerning travelers year-round, Miami's visitor numbers are stronger and more stable than ever. Now, Miami's always in season!

The "press and public relations" line item in the 2003 state tourism budgets showed an average actual budget of $258,686. Other PR-related average actual budget line items in the survey included domestic and international advertising ($3.5 million), sales promotion ($1.5 million), printing and production ($520,756), and Web site development/maintenance ($247,385). The state offices are especially effective in advertising destinations and their tourist attractions, representing the latter at national and international travel trade shows, and operating "welcome centers." Some state offices also have specialists to work with motion picture studios on "on-location film shootings."

PR practitioners at the state tourism offices, and the CVBs they support, also do a very effective job in facilitating the visits of travel writers and the media to local destinations and tourist attractions.

WORKING WITH TRAVEL WRITERS

State travel offices and CVBs rely strongly on coverage from travel writers to promote their destinations. Almost all of the offices and bureaus employ a senior practitioner to handle relations with the media. While many writers visit on their own because they have a definite assignment from a news media outlet, they contact PR professionals for information about local lodging, sightseeing, and dining attractions. This is especially true of freelancers, who often have no budget to finance their research and writing. Writers from major newspapers such as *The New York Times* and influential magazines such as *Conde Nast Traveler* are prohibited by their editors from accepting complimentary treatment, but they still appreciate destination suggestions from PR representatives. (See Appendix F, Planning Press Trips That Pay Off.)

One of the most difficult decisions for state tourism and CVB PR practitioners is whether to host or "comp" visits by free-lancers without definite assignments. If the writer has a solid track record of past placements, hosting the writer can be a ben-eficial long-term investment that often results in coverage later on. Membership in the Society of American Travel Writers (SATW) is one reliable indicator of whether a freelancer is a legitimate journalist—but this is not foolproof. Asking a free-lancer to provide samples of past work is a standard best prac-tice. Those writers who are notorious for seeking free accommodations, and who are not producing, usually end up on "Do Not Host" lists that are shared by experienced PR prac-titioners.

A common method for bringing journalists to a destination is the press or familiarization ("fam") trip. These trips frequently are conducted to coincide with a destination's major celebration such as New Orleans' Mardi Gras or Washington, D.C.'s Cherry Blossom Festival. Experienced attraction PR people will have solid relationships with their local CVB peers and will be given the opportunity to host visiting groups of writers on their premises.

There are many media that write about destinations and attrac-tions. The travel and meeting trade publications cover destina-tions for specialized audiences of travel agents and meeting planners. Many foreign newspapers and magazines visit attrac-tions such as Florida's beaches, Los Angeles' Hollywood, or the Grand Canyon to inform their readers about what to expect on their trips to these popular attractions. The Travel Channel, CNN, Arts & Entertainment, PBS, Food, and other cable TV outlets also produce in-depth pieces on destinations and attrac-tions. The principal PR tools for reaching all of these news media are Web sites, B-roll, press kits, CD-ROMs, videos, and promotional brochures.

THE NEW "NICHE TRAVELER" MARKET

Destination PR practitioners constantly seek to impress freelance writers for such popular guidebooks as *Fodor's, Frommer's,* and *The Lonely Planet*. Writers of these guides, of course, require more details on prices, transportation modes, and historical facts. Many of these guides have recently begun to publish books appealing to "niche travelers" such as hikers, cyclists, women, families, pet lovers, and gay and lesbian travelers.

An example of the special focus on the latter group appeared in the July 3, 2004, edition of *The Washington Post*. The article described a new campaign launched by the Greater Philadelphia Tourism Marketing Corp. aimed specifically at gay tourists. This group spends $54 billion per year, or an average of $500 per two-day domestic trip. A TV ad in the campaign featured this tagline: "Come to Philadelphia. Get your history straight and your nightlife gay."

Many destinations and attractions today try to capitalize on popular trends in their PR efforts. For example, there is the recent strong trend toward "experiential travel"—which refers to interactive hands-on experiences. One of the innovators in this category was Colonial Williamsburg (Va.) where for years they have invited visitors to take part in 18th-century activities such as glassblowing, bookbinding, blacksmithing, and meat curing. In the Berkshires area of western Massachusetts, visitors today can follow routes that feature farming, apple- and cherry-picking, cidermaking, crafts-making, and festival participation. (See Sidebar 5-2, "Cooperstown—More Than a Baseball Town.")

SIDEBAR 5-2
COOPERSTOWN (N.Y.)—MORE THAN
A BASEBALL TOWN
BY NANCY JO FRIEDMAN, PRESIDENT
NANCY J. FRIEDMAN PUBLIC RELATIONS
NEW YORK, N.Y.

Hear Cooperstown, think baseball. Historically overshadowed and best known for the Baseball Hall of Fame, the village of Cooperstown, N.Y., is far less known for its other compelling attributes. Small-town American charm, unique cultural attractions, and pristine Lake Otsego also define the destination. In the past, the majority of visitors came on a pilgrimage to the Baseball Hall of Fame, bypassing the "other" Cooperstown. Those tunnel-visioned visitors were blinded from other local delights like the living history Farmers' Museum, the Fenimore Art Museum, the Glimmerglass Opera, the Otesaga resort, the Cooper Inn, and the Leatherstocking Golf Course on the shores of Lake Otsego.

A public relations campaign was established to remedy this perception by building awareness of this charming, one-of-a-kind village and all it has to offer. Outreach was targeted to specific market segments including families, golfers, couples (romance, honeymoon, weekend getaways), groups and meetings seeking a unique venue, as well as culture lovers. The destination was positioned as a slice of "pure Americana," rich in literary heritage and offering something for everyone whether or not baseball was of interest.

The press kit was designed to showcase the village's bucolic nature by using Janet Munro's representational painting of the village supplied by the Fenimore Art Museum/New York State Historical Association. Logos representing the best of Cooperstown were included on letterhead and in the kit to reinforce there's more than baseball.

A comprehensive but highly targeted media relations program commenced, which incorporated one-on-one story pitching, both individual and group press visits, issuing of news releases, and attending various media marketplaces sponsored by Historic Hotels of America and the Society of American Travel Writers.

The focus was specific. It included the New York State drive-to market for association and small convention business, as well as family, general, golf, and cultural travel. Since most previous coverage about Cooperstown had been baseball related, the opportunities were wide open to invite the chronicling of this surprising village. The campaign resulted in extensive coverage, which included features entitled, "Yes, America, There Really Is A Cooperstown" in *Travel & Leisure* magazine; "American Pastoral" in *Town & Country;* "Art For Kids' Sake" in *Family Fun;* "Yuletide Road Trips" in *Martha Stewart Living;* "Myths & Legends" in the *Houston Chronicle;* and multiple features in the meeting trades. The Leatherstocking Golf Course and the Otesaga Hotel was named one of the 50 Best Golf Resorts in *Conde Nast Traveler* and golf features ran in *Golf Digest, Golf for Women, Links* and many others. For the first time, the bridal books included Cooperstown, as did regional magazines such as *Connecticut, Boston,* and *Yankee,* and airline in-flight, *Delta Sky*. Twice *The New York Times* published a "What's Doing in Cooperstown" feature in the Sunday Travel section and most major papers in the northeast wrote about the destination, from *The Boston*

Globe to the *Baltimore Sun, Philadelphia Inquirer,* and *Newsday*.

After 9/11, the destination, which "oozed" Americana, was used in a number of national advertising campaigns seeking to capitalize on the way life used to be in more "innocent" times. This trend was suggested to *USA Today,* which then published a feature entitled, " 'Perfect Village' Cooperstown Scores" focusing on how its clean, American image was used to market other products.

When a local old age home burned down during a renovation and the elderly residents were housed at the Otesaga Resort, displacing revenue business for a year, coverage was secured on NBC's *Today Show* in a four-minute segment placing charity over commerce on Christmas Day. This same story ran on the Associated Press wire and was picked up by dozens of major news outlets across the country.

Some journalists wrote sentimental pieces on their pilgrimage to Cooperstown to fulfill a dying parent's wish and these kinds of personal experience stories often won awards for the deep connection the town inspired between parent and child. Prior to the Hall of Fame inductions every summer, the Agency would reach out to the local home town city paper of the inductee to solicit coverage about the destination with the local angle of the home town team's hero getting inducted.

Bookings and museum attendance rose by 30 percent following the initiation of the campaign. Some years, call volume rose by more than 50 percent. Because of the increased demand, the season at the Otesaga Hotel was extended by a few weeks each year until it stayed open through Thanksgiving and then finally opened for group business in the winter. The targeted public relations outreach was effective in making the destination better known, more visible, and more appealing to a variety of audiences. Many of the media "hits" were home runs, which benefited America' s most perfect village.

The National Park Service

Although the U.S. government no longer operates a top level national tourism agency (see Chapter 1), one federal organization that remains a key player in America's destination/tourist attraction activity is the U.S. National Park Service (NPS), an agency of the Department of the Interior. The NPS operates on an annual budget of approximately $2 billion.

NPS was established in 1916 and today manages 52 national parks in 27 states. California and Alaska have the most parks, each with eight. Yellowstone, in Montana and Wyoming, is the oldest park, and most famous for its "Old Faithful" geyser. According to the NPS, the parks attracted 266 million visitors in 2003. Among the most visited parks (with 2 million or more annual visitors) were the Great Smokey Mountains (Tennessee and North Carolina), Grand Canyon (Arizona), Cuyahoga Valley (Ohio), Olympic (Washington), Yosemite (California), Rocky Mountain (Colorado), Yellowstone (Montana and Wyoming), Acadia (Maine), and Zion (Utah).

Of special note is that NPS oversight today extends to much more than the national parks. Under the title "National Park System," this oversight covers monuments, battlefields, military parks, historic sites, lakeshores, seashores, recreation areas, scenic rivers and trails, and the White House.

The Importance of Truth in Crisis Communications

Just as in the other three major travel and tourism sectors, destination and attraction PR practitioners must contend with various crises. Every fall, beach destinations along the Gulf and Atlantic coasts are threatened by hurricanes.

The aftermath of destruction to many Florida and Caribbean island resorts from hurricanes Frances, Jeanne, and Ivan in the fall of 2004 should demonstrate to destination officials why it is so imperative to have a crisis communications plan, and to closely adhere to that plan. But beyond that, the string of three hurricanes proved to be an object lesson of the PR damage that can occur when you compel your PR representatives to cover up the facts about the real extent of the damage.

Unfortunately, a number of destination/attraction officials during the hurricane crises were reluctant to fully disclose all of the facts about local damage and closings, for fear of losing future business. As a result, the news media and prospective guests received inaccurate and mixed messages about the status of affected destinations. And these officials may never be able to recover from their lost credibility with those audiences.

The fundamental lesson for destination officials to learn from the hurricanes is this: *In a crisis of any kind, tell the truth and tell it quickly.* Otherwise you risk irreparable damage to your business reputation and you render your future PR efforts ineffective.

TOUR OPERATORS AND WHOLESALERS

Tour operators and wholesalers comprise a fundamental audience not only for destinations and attractions, but also for all of the major sectors of travel and tourism. These operators basically assemble travel itinerary packages that often offer the best value made possible by high volume business. The packages generally include escorted air transportation and accommodations, but may also include meals, ground transportation, excursions, and entertainment. The tour wholesalers contract with airlines and hotels for a set number of seats and rooms, receiving a quantity discount. Retail travel agents sell these tour packages, receiving a commission from the wholesalers. Many of the wholesalers are members of the U.S. Tour Operators Association (USTOA) or the National Tour Association (NTA).

The trend in recent years has been toward more specialized tours rather than general ones—specialized from the standpoint of both price range and experience level. The latter coincides with the emergence of new types of "niche tourism," and the growing popularity of packaged trips related to educational interests, reunions, sports events, and gay and lesbian travel. Ideal forums for the major industry sectors to make contact with tour operators are the large annual trade shows in the United States and abroad.

Operators are quick to capitalize on popular lifestyle trends when organizing their tours. For example, taking off on the spate of recent TV crime investigation shows, one clever wholesaler recently announced a crime-forensic tour featuring classes in finger printing and blood-spatter analysis. Another operator is selling tours that follow routes cited in the best-selling novel *The Da Vinci Code*.

"Niche Tourism"

Some of the most prevalent tourism niches today are adventure travel, agritourism, geo/ecotourism, heritage/cultural tourism, and volunteer tourism.

Adventure Travel

Adventure travel refers mostly to outdoor sporting activities, and can include everything from whitewater rafting, cycling tours, ranch vacations, and African safaris, to hiking, mountain climbing, fishing, camping, boating, skiing, hot-air ballooning, and whale-watching. A major boost for this niche has come from the national obsession with health and physical fitness. A subset of this niche is "soft adventure," which connotes less strenuous activities that are tailored for many traveling seniors and those who are less physically fit.

AGRITOURISM

Agritourism is centered primarily on experiencing life on working farms through activities such as collecting eggs, feeding livestock, picking fruit, planting crops, etc. One prominent example of these offerings is the Pennsylvania Dutch Country. Another good example is the Hudson River Valley of New York, where tourists can enjoy a farm-to-table experience at the Stone Barns Center for Food and Agriculture in Pocantico Hills. Another Hudson Valley attraction is the campus of the Culinary Institute of America in Hyde Park.

GEOTOURISM AND ECOTOURISM

Geotourism and ecotourism are closely related and refer to travel that enhances the geographical character of a place or explores the ecological beauty of flora and fauna in a particular area. Prominent examples include all of the U.S. National Parks. The proliferation of expansive new aquariums across the country is another example of this special interest.

HERITAGE/CULTURAL TOURISM

Heritage/cultural tourism concentrates on the historical and cultural sites that abound throughout the nation, including theaters, museums, and science centers. Prime examples in Virginia include Colonial Williamsburg, George Washington's home at Mount Vernon, and Thomas Jefferson's home, Monticello, near Charlottesville.

VOLUNTEER TOURISM

More and more people are traveling today to participate in volunteer community service and humanitarian projects. These include programs to improve natural, historic, and cultural resources, archeological excavations, and national park improvements. The Habitat for Humanity program that builds new homes for needy families is a typical example of this volunteerism movement.

PR FOR AMUSEMENT/THEME PARKS AND ATTRACTIONS

A significant segment of the destinations/attractions sector of travel and tourism is the 600 U.S. amusement/theme parks and attractions where more than 300 million people take more than 1.5 billion rides per year. The 600 facilities include zoos, aquariums, museums and historic sites, water parks, and family entertainment centers. The primary audience for this vast segment is leisure travelers seeking family fun and entertainment, recreational, or educational experiences.

The principal organization representing most of these diverse components is the International Association of Amusement Parks and Attractions (IAAPA). Based in Alexandria, Va., this group is comprised of more than 5,000 members worldwide. Its main responsibilities include communications, advocacy, education and resources, and annual trade shows and conventions.

IAAPA's nine-person communications department includes a director and a staff to handle media relations, technical and news writing, Web site maintenance, and publication production. In addition to its consumer-driven Web site, IAAPA communicates with its members and consumers through a monthly in-house publication titled *FUNWORLD*.

While the largest amusement/theme parks, and the largest attractions, have full in-house PR staffs, many of the smaller parks and attractions rely on media relations support from IAAPA—especially in the area of crisis communications. The most prevalent messages communicated to the media include the following: the park industry's 99.9 percent safety record; industry statistics; new technologies such as online ticketing systems; new rides, attractions, and exhibits; and food offerings.

IAAPA notes a trend in the increased popularity in the United States of indoor water parks that are connected to hotel properties and feature river runs, slides, and wave pools.

One of the least likely categories of tourist attractions (and one not under the IAAPA umbrella) is shopping centers—especially the scores of discount outlet store malls that dot the countryside. The massive Potomac Mills complex in the suburbs of Northern Virginia is one notable example. In a category of its own is The Mall of America in Bloomington, Minn., which is not only a tourist attraction, but also bills itself as "the largest indoor family theme park." The Mall includes over 500 stores, 60 restaurants, dozens of rides, nightclubs, and an aquarium. It reports 40 million visitors per year—40 percent of whom it categorizes as tourists.

Amusement parks occasionally experience mechanical breakdowns of their rides that may lead to injuries or deaths. And due to homeland terrorism threats, many attractions have had to implement sometimes distracting security measures at their facilities to ensure public safety. All of these circumstances require constant vigilance and comprehensive crisis communications plans.

For more information on attractions, state tourism efforts, and destinations, readers should contact the following organizations, which all operate under the umbrella of TIA: the National Council of Attractions, the National Council of State Tourism Directors, and the National Council of Destination Organizations. Other prime sources are the International Association of Amusement Parks and Attractions (IAAPA) and the Destination Marketing Association International (DMAI). (See Sidebar 5-3, "Customizing 'The Mouse'—Or How Disney Found Success with the Business Press.")

SIDEBAR 5-3
CUSTOMIZING "THE MOUSE"—OR HOW DISNEY FOUND SUCCESS WITH THE BUSINESS PRESS
BY VICKI JOHNSON, COMMUNICATIONS & DEVELOPMENT DIRECTOR SALES & TRAVEL OPERATIONS, WALT DISNEY PARKS AND RESORTS ORLANDO, FLORIDA

For more than 75 years, people all over the world have associated the Disney brand with fantasy and pixie dust experiences. It can truly be considered one of the iconic brands in the international corporate community.

Getting the business media to really understand how Disney reaches its decisions on pricing our theme park product took a lot more effort than just sprinkling pixie dust on our press releases. Finding a way to generate positive, and accurate, coverage with the business press is another Disney success story.

While it all began with a mouse named Mickey, the empire grew from releasing the first full-length animated feature ("Snow White") to a corporate conglomerate. Today it operates resort destinations on three continents. In September 2005, that number will grow again when Hong Kong Disneyland opens. The Disney Cruise line is a major player in the family cruise business, and Disney theme parks occupy 10 of the top 15 spots on the *Amusement Business* list of the world's most visited theme parks.

New Ticket Pricing Spurs New Media Strategy

The Walt Disney World public relations team has always enjoyed excellent access to "A-list" travel media around the world. We have conducted many media outreach efforts timed to new openings and initiatives, but with success, and access, came a certain amount of skepticism and scrutiny from the influential business media.

This was especially true when it came to the sensitive issue of pricing and admission costs for Disney attractions. Any raise in prices focused on the higher cost of a single-day ticket admission to one park, rather than on the more usual consumer practice of purchasing multi-day tickets to the four Walt Disney World theme Parks—the Magic Kingdom, Epcot, Disney-MGM Studios, and Disney's Animal Kingdom.

The Walt Disney World PR team decided on a more targeted approach when debuting new pricing programs. We hoped to avoid business journalists writing stories relying solely upon the speculation of travel industry "experts" and stock analysts about the effect on Disney and its customers. Invariably, the resulting articles focused on changes to single-day ticket prices, rather than explaining increased prices were tied to new attractions, shows, and services. The revised media strategy kicked off with the introduction of "Magic Your Way Vacations," and emphasized the flexibility and affordability of the new program.

THIRD-PARTY SUPPORT INSURES BEST PRESS COVERAGE

The key to gaining more positive, and accurate, business coverage included networking with unbiased, third-party travel experts, and making sure they were totally aware of the advantages of the "Magic Your Way Vacations," including a reduction in the actual per-day cost of theme park ticket prices. Their advance awareness of the program, and how it worked, included giving them access to Disney executives, who explained the hows and whys of this new vacation initiative. While it did not "buy" Disney favorable press coverage, it did make those travel analysts, and experts, who are consulted by the media better informed, prior to being contacted for comment by the business reporters.

Following the announcement to the media of "Magic Your Way Vacations," the resulting coverage was far more positive. Headlines included "Disney World Creates Flexible Ticketing Policy" and "Customizing the Mouse: Disney Reveals Pricing Change." The third party experts' comments were much more positive and accurate about the impact on consumers and Disney's bottom line.

Contacting travel experts in advance, and making certain they understood the business rationale behind Walt Disney World's new ticket pricing strategy, showed the power and credibility of third-party endorsements, even with a skeptical business press. It has been a public relations success story for Disney.

6

What Travel and Tourism Employers Should Understand About PR

Above all, travel and tourism employers should recognize that PR by itself is not an immediate panacea for solving all of your image problems. It has a much better chance of succeeding if you give it time to build solid long-term relationships with your firm's key audiences. You can help your practitioners be successful by insuring that they are constantly "kept in the loop"—keep them fully apprised of company developments and grant them direct access to your top executives. Lastly, always remember that no amount of PR can overcome a flawed or unsafe product or service. As the old adage goes: "You can' t make a silk purse out of a sow's ear!" If you try to use PR to cover up serious deficiencies, your efforts are doomed to fail, because PR becomes impotent once it loses its credibility.

THE VALUE OF PR

It is difficult (but not impossible) to give a precise value to PR. The big question many experts have struggled with is: How do you measure the monetary value of achieving goodwill among target audiences?

The practice, however, is moving toward more systematic measurement of its results. Presently, some of the most common measurement systems entail the following: *media impressions,* based on the numbers of people exposed to a message; *advertising equivalency,* based on column inches generated from free publicity in print media versus advertising costs for equivalent space; *Internet hits* on a Web site; *numbers of news clippings* from targeted media; or *surveying results against original objectives.* Some PR firms have developed more refined formulas for measuring results, but this information often is proprietary and not generally available to all practitioners.

The question of PR's value basically comes down to significant intangibles. For example, the noted University of Maryland professor and author James E. Grunig says in his book *Excellence in Public Relations and Communications Management:* "The major purpose of PR is to save money for the organization by building relations with publics that constrain or enhance the ability of the organization to meet its mission."

In his hospitality marketing book *Heads in Beds,* Ivo Raza says publicity is more valuable than advertising in communicating messages because it is PR that best creates the launch of a brand. This is true because of PR's greater credibility, which comes from third-party endorsement of messages by the media when it uses the messages. Raza also points out that PR is quite inexpensive compared to advertising. These same truths are expressed in the Al and Laura Ries book *The Fall of Advertising and the Rise of PR.*

Other ways PR saves the company money are by paving the way for sales, fundraising, and stock offerings through publicity campaigns; building employees' morale and gaining their acceptance of change through employee communications; providing early warning of issues through close monitoring of news developments; influencing public policy through lobbying; and preserving the company's reputation and stock price through pro-active crisis communications planning.

Hiring an In-House Practitioner

The trend today is to operate smaller in-house PR departments, and to outsource for specialized PR services. But if you decide you want to hire an in-house practitioner, experts agree these are the fundamental skills that will be most valuable:

1. Excellent communications abilities—both written and verbal.

2. Strong media relations and media contacts.

3. Creativity; an idea person.

4. Strategic planner or pro-active thinker.

5. Ability to work under pressure on stringent media deadlines.

6. Sound judgment.

In addition, you should specify a preference for someone with experience in travel and tourism or in your particular sector of the industry. The education requirement and number of years of experience of course depends on the level of the position.

One way to identify qualified candidates is to ascertain if they are members of the two largest professional organizations—the Public Relations Society of America (PRSA) and the International Association of Business Communicators (IABC)—and if they are fully accredited as professionals by those groups. For example, PRSA members who have passed the demanding requisite exams for accreditation are entitled to use the APR (Accredited in Public Relations) designation after their names. Another alternative to consider is contacting local universities and colleges that offer PR studies to identify qualified interns who could temporarily lighten your PR workload or who you could groom for a permanent position.

To fill a new, permanent position, be sure to contact these sources: the PRSA and IABC chapter offices closest to you (most of these provide their members with Jobline services); the PR offices of your key industry professional/trade associations; local colleges and universities that offer PR degree programs or noncredit certificate programs; or *PR Week,* a major PR trade publication based in New York City.

EMPLOYING OUTSIDE PR FIRMS/CONSULTANTS

Depending on your circumstances, you may want to hire an outside firm or consultant to perform all of your PR functions full time, to handle a major, one-time project such as a grand opening, or to provide specialized services that exceed the expertise or capability of your in-house practitioner. Some of the most common specialized services sought by businesses include executive media training, crisis communications, financial/investor relations, international or nationwide PR, large-scale audiovisual presentations, speechwriting, lobbying, and corporate identification programs.

Three excellent sources for identifying PR firms that specialize in travel and tourism issues are:

1. PRSA's annual *Red Book Directory,* which lists agencies that claim travel and tourism as an industry specialty. Note that in 2004 PRSA folded this book into its overall membership directory.

2. *O'Dwyer's Annual Directory of PR Firms,* which lists U.S. agencies by location and specialty. Periodically, *O'Dwyer's* publishes a special supplement entitled *Profiles of Travel PR Firms.*

3. The Council of Public Relations Firms—go to its Web site at www.prfirms.org and click the Find-a-Firm page.

WHAT YOU SHOULD KNOW ABOUT THE RFP PROCESS

Once you have identified a number of potential PR firms that could help, you are ready to engage in the Request for Proposal (RFP) process. This is where you put out a call for written details on how these firms would address your challenge and what their costs would be. Great care should be exercised in preparing the RFP so that all the bidders clearly understand what you expect. Begin by describing the challenge you face, and provide some background on your company and its culture. Next, state your objectives. Then explain what you see as the scope of the job, what your key messages should be, what kind of results you seek, and specify the time frame, deadlines, and overall budget range.

There are a number of additional requirements you can specify in your RFP. For example, you can ask for the proposal to be split in several parts, requesting a number of different time frames and services envisioned under each, along with the costs under each scenario. You also may want to specify that you expect the PR firm to assign a full-time representative to work full-time at the company's headquarters for the duration of the contract. Finally, it is always wise to ask for detailed timelines and periodic written progress reports.

After the RFPs have been issued, you may want to set up some sort of internal company panel to review and rate the proposals received in order to narrow down the field to a manageable number of finalists. Written proposals may run from just a few pages in a simple folder, to hundreds of pages in a glossy binder, with photos, magazine reprints, newspaper clippings, CDs, videotapes, and testimonial letters attached. Typical contents include background on the PR firm and its principals; the names and biographies of those executives who will be assigned to your account; an outline of proposed services and programs to be implemented and their cost estimates; and lists of present and past clients (mostly those whom the firm served under assignments similar to yours).

Selecting the Best Proposal for Your Organization

When examining the written proposals, these are some of the points on which you want your panelists to focus: Does the firm outline innovative programs and services to address your objectives? (Regarding this question, keep in mind that many PR firms are reluctant to disclose their most creative ideas in their proposals.

You will have to judge their creativity from personal references and past performance.)

Other aspects for panelists to consider: Are the services and results promised feasible or exaggerated? Has the firm demonstrated successful experience with clients who had PR needs similar to you? Have the executives to be assigned to your account had in-depth experience in dealing with clients with PR challenges comparable to your own, and how much of their time will be devoted to your account? You will of course want to check the firm's client list for references and to rule out potential conflicts of interest with your business.

At this point it is appropriate to ask the finalists to "pitch" the account at formal, in-person presentations to your panel on your premises. This is often where the firms will attempt to "pull out all of the stops" to impress and dazzle the panel members. This is also your chance to evaluate how compatible those executives to be assigned to your account are with your staff and your corporate culture. It is also the time to ask tough follow-up questions generated by the written proposals and to clarify points that were unclear. Above all, do not let slick and dazzling presentations cloud your judgment. And remember, bigger firms are not always the best! Following the presentation, you should have your panel give a final rating to each finalist, and then expeditiously announce the winner.

Finally, keep in mind that outside PR firms—although they may be able to provide an objective point of view that may be necessary, specialized services beyond your capability, and extensive experience beyond your geographic vicinity—do not possess intimate knowledge of your organization and its leaders, and they undoubtedly will be more expensive than an internal practitioner. Some typical cost factors used by most agencies are listed in the following section.

PR FIRM COMPENSATION

Fees for *continuing services* are established one of three ways:

1. A monthly retainer covering a fixed number of hours and services.

2. A minimum retainer, plus monthly billing for actual staff time at hourly rates on a per diem basis.

3. Straight hourly charges.

Fees for special projects are paid on an hourly basis or on a negotiated fixed fee covering the full project. (Such projects are usually the most labor intensive.)

Out of pocket expenses are generally billed at cost and are exclusive of the retainer fee.

On average, for a small- to medium-size account, clients can expect to work with a PR firm's team typically composed of a senior account supervisor (AS), an account executive (AE), an assistant account executive (AAE), and junior support staff. Hourly fees may range from a low of $25 an hour for AAEs and junior support staff to several hundred dollars per hour for the AE, AS, and firm principals.

A PROMISING FUTURE

The 21st century should see U.S. travel and tourism PR experience significant growth. The principal trend driving the industry's success will be the aging of the American society. Baby boomers are nearing 60 and dominate society. Households headed by people over 55 are the fastest-growing segment of America's consumer market, and this group controls an increasing percentage of all personal income. This group typically has more inherited wealth and discretionary income, which is expected to be spent on travel.

Industry experts predict that the segment that will most benefit from this trend is luxury travel—particularly high-end hotels and their residences and the booming cruise ship business. Certain segments of niche tourism are also expected to be large beneficiaries of this trend—especially such niches as "experiential" (featuring adventure and how-to-do-it experiences), cultural, and "reunion tourism" (appealing to families and social groups).

As this book goes to press, the trend toward increased luxury amenities in the hotel sector, as a result of the growing influence of the affluent baby boomer population, was gaining momentum in some of the industry's other major sectors—especially the transportation sector. This trend toward new "pampering" services was very evident aboard many cruise ships. It also was a recurring theme in the airline business, where carriers were making plans for a generation of larger, multi-deck planes that might offer in-flight amenities such as spa treatments and gambling casinos. As long as favorable economic conditions continue, this new emphasis on expensive luxury service and comfort can be expected to flourish and spread throughout all of the industry's major sectors.

In-bound and out-bound tourism involving some Eastern European and Asian countries is expected to surge. Mainland China, in particular, with its 1.3 billion population and its 3 million-square-mile area filled with cultural attractions, should become a focal point for expanded tourist traffic.

The 21st century could also see the advent of sub-orbital space tourist travel—initial round-trip cost estimates per person are $200,000. NASA and private industry are aiming for this eventuality, and private industry already has designed and successfully test-launched its own spaceship for tourists.

All of these developments and trends are good news for the industry and PR practitioners in travel and tourism. Barring any more catastrophic events such as the 9/11 terrorist attacks in New York City, the Pentagon, and Pennsylvania, opportunities for industry PR practitioners in the new century appear to be abundant.

Appendix A

Selected Travel and Tourism Professional/Trade Associations

Air Transport Association (ATA)
1301 Pennsylvania Ave., NW, Suite 1100
Washington, D.C. 20004-1707
202-626-4172
www.airlines.org

American Association of Museums (AAM)
1575 I St., NW, Suite 400
Washington, D.C. 20005
202-289-1818
www.aam-us.org

American Automobile Association (AAA)
1000 AAA Drive
Heathrow, Fla. 32746
407-444-7188
www.aaanewsroom.net

American Bus Association (ABA)
1100 New York Ave., Suite 1050
Washington, D.C.
202-218-7223
www.buses.org

American Hotel & Lodging Association (AHLA)
1201 New York Ave., NW, #60
Washington, D.C. 20005-3931
202-289-3100
www.ahla.com

American Society of Travel Agents (ASTA)
1101 King St.
Alexandria, Va. 22314
703-739-8707
www.astanet.com

Cruise Lines International Association (CLIA)
80 Broad St., Suite 180
New York, N.Y. 10004
212-921-0066
www.cruising.org

Destination Marketing Association International (DMAI)
2025 M St., NW, Suite 500
Washington, D.C. 20036
202-835-4205
www.iacvb.org

Hotel Sales & Marketing Association International (HSMAI)
8201 Greensboro Dr., Suite 200
McLean, Va. 21202
703-610-9024
www.hsmai.org

International Association of Amusement Parks & Attractions
   (IAAPA)
1448 Duke St.
Alexandria. Va. 22314
703-836-4800
www.iaapa.org

International Council of Cruise Lines (ICCL)
2111 Wilson Blvd., 8th floor
Arlington, Va. 22201
703-522-8463
www.iccl.org

International Hotel and Restaurant Association (IH & RA)
48 boulevard de Sebastopol
75003, Paris, France
33 1 44 88 92 20
www.ih-ra.com

Meeting Professionals International (MPI)
4455 LBJ Freeway
Dallas, Tex. 75244-5903
972-703-3000
www.mpiweb.org

National Business Travel Association (NBTA)
110 North Royal St., 4th floor
Alexandria, Va. 22314
703-684-0386
www.nbta.org

National Restaurant Association (NRA)
1200 17th St., NW
Washington, D.C. 20036
202-331-5900
www.restaurant.org

National Tour Association (NTA)
546 East Main St.
Lexington, Ky. 40508
859-226-4444
www.ntaonline.com

Professional Association of Innkeepers International (PAII)
16 South Haddon Ave.
Haddonfield, N.J. 08033
856-354-0030
www.paii.org

Public Relations Society of America (PRSA) Travel & Tourism
    Section
33 Maiden Lane, 11th Floor
New York, N.Y. 10038
212-460-1400
www.prsa.org

Recreation Vehicle Industry Association (RVIA)
1896 Preston White Drive
Reston, Va. 20191
703-620-6003
www.rvia.com

Society of American Travel Writers (SATW)
1500 Sunday Drive, Suite 102
Raleigh, N.C. 27607
919-861-5586
www.satw.org

Travel Industry Association of America (TIA)
1100 New York Ave., NW, Suite 450
Washington, D.C. 20005-3934
202-408-8422
www.tia.org

U.S. Tour Operators Association (USTOA)
275 Madison Ave., Suite 2014
New York, N.Y. 10016
212-599-6599
www.ustoa.com

World Tourism Organization (WTO)
Capitan Haya 42
28020 Madrid, Spain
Tel: (34) 91-567-81-00
www.worldtourism.org/index.htm

Appendix B

The Travel Industry's PR Response to 9/11

Remarks by Dexter Koehl,
Vice President, Public Relations & Communications,
Travel Industry Association of America at
TOURCOM, Madrid, Spain, Friday, January 30, 2004

Every one of us in the U.S. travel industry remembers where we were on September 11th, what it felt like to see the terrible attacks, and what it was like to manage a travel organization in the immediate aftermath.

While much of the nation could wait for the shock to subside, we had to move immediately into crisis management mode. I am going to share with you how Travel Industry Association of America staff assembled the travel industry's troops and launched a *ten-week counter offensive* literally before the smoke had cleared.

Almost immediately after the news had set in on September 11th TIA President and CEO Bill Norman began to consult with members of TIA's 15-person executive committee and a Travel Industry Recovery Coalition was formed representing 26 sectors of the U.S. travel and tourism industry. A message and battle plan quickly followed. We knew where we had to go and we had a plan to get there.

Week One: By September 17th the TIA senior staff team had created and begun to execute a recovery plan with two major goals: *Ensure safe, secure travel.* And *restore travelers' confidence.* We needed to be unified as an industry. And we needed to bring as many other industry groups and the federal government on board with us.

Our first target was the news media. We had to seize the moment in the media and we did. As you would expect, the media were hungry for statistics, forecasts, literally anything they could get their hands on with regard to our industry. We recognized an opportunity to provide the industry with *one voice, one message,* and *the tools to deliver that message*.

We gathered more than 50 of the top PR and communications professionals in the travel industry via conference call and presented a *common message and strategy,* with all the tools to implement a unified industry PR campaign.

Our message platform was clear and simple: *"Travel is a fundamental American freedom.* We as an industry have a duty and responsibility to preserve and protect that freedom. We support the government's efforts to enhance safety and we as an industry must work together to restore consumer confidence in the safety of the U.S. travel product."

We provided talking points, facts and figures, sample letters to the editor, and other materials in a *special micro-site* on the TIA web site, www.tia.org. It became an easily accessible source for response for the industry.

The micro-site was an industry media clearinghouse that communicated to the U.S. and international media our availability as a source for timely information about the industry.

Over and over the public heard our message: Travel is a fundamental American freedom. A return to travel is a return to normalcy.

Week Two: While our public relations campaign was underway, we were setting up our next phase—a national newspaper advertising campaign.

Our ad agency held two focus groups, one in New York City and one in the state of Ohio, and created several ads within 10 days of the incident. What we learned was that consumers wanted to know what the industry was doing about safety and security. Consumers wanted an industry message to reassure them that things were being done to make it safe to travel. In addition, they made it clear that they expected a "deal" or an offer to get them back.

Week Three: TIA went ahead with its previously scheduled annual Marketing Outlook Forum in Atlanta with a revised agenda and communications tools for TIA members. This was an ideal setting to meet with almost 500 senior marketing executives and communicate our crisis strategy and message face to face. The timing could not be better—proving that sometimes luck is on your side.

We also launched the first round of national advertising October 2nd in eight newspaper markets across the country. The ad was clean, simple and had a strong impact. Let me read it to you:

> *We see America as a land where the freedom to come and go as we please is a cherished right.*
>
> *That's why America's travel industry has pledged its full support to the U.S. Congress and other federal agencies to ensure that travel is safe and secure.*
>
> *After all, America was founded, expanded and made great by travelers.*
>
> *And nobody can take that away from us.*
>
> *Not now. Not ever.*

At the very bottom of the ad it said:

> *SeeAmerica.org is a web portal to all U.S. travel industry sites supported by the Travel Industry Association of America, a non-profit organization representing all segments of the U.S. travel industry.*

In addition to the paid advertising, the ad ran as editorial in newspapers around the country. The ad launched a comprehensive advertising and public service announcement or PSA campaign using *SeeAmerica* as a unifying brand.

SeeAmerica.org is a non-profit, non-commercial consumer web site that links to every travel industry organization in the U.S. It is a one-stop Internet location designed to get travelers to every travel site in America: cities, states, and companies.

This SeeAmerica.org web site and the SeeAmerica brand name had been promoted the previous year in the UK, Japan, and

Brazil. It now played an important role in linking the industry together domestically.

Week Four: The next advertising component was an advertising template with the message, "It's your country. See it. SeeAmerica." Our members downloaded this art from TIA's business-to-business web site, tia.org, and wrapped it around their own advertising messages.

We created a print public service announcement campaign for newspapers and magazines and for members to use in their own publications. It simply stated, "It's your Country, See it. SeeAmerica.org."

TIA member *USA Today* donated $1 million in media value to promote recovery through SeeAmerica advertising. Full page ads appeared in *USA Today* and banner ads ran on usatoday.com, their online web edition.

The template campaign then transitioned to a second phase as the Christmas holiday season approached. It centered on the theme of "give the gift of travel this holiday season."

Week Five: We remained focused on using the national brand, SeeAmerica, to leverage limited resources. Whether it was simply using the SeeAmerica logo in their ads or adopting the whole campaign, the industry benefited by leveraging our resources.

Week Six: The U.S. National Parks and Forests announced that they would not charge entrance fees on Veterans' Day, the November 11 national holiday, to honor the sacrifices veterans had made.

We built on their idea and created SeeAmerica Day, as a Veterans' Day holiday promotion to encourage Americans to see their country, visit their monuments, visit friends—in short, we wanted to get people moving. We solicited offers throughout the industry to post on the SeeAmerica web site and then we announced it through a pictorial e-mail. This allowed us to make a national announcement quickly and at no cost. The e-mail was sent to all of TIA's 2,000 member organizations who, in turn, sent it to their customers, vendors and employees announcing their special offers.

Many cities in America offered free transportation, free entrance to museums and monuments or highly discounted rates for SeeAmerica Day. Hotel companies offered special SeeAmerica rates and some airlines did the same. And all of the offers were listed on the SeeAmerica web site with direct links to the site where the offer could be purchased.

Week Nine: Our most visible crisis communications effort came in week nine with a television ad campaign featuring President Bush and *real travel industry workers*.

Our industry owes an enormous debt of gratitude to Bill Marriott, chairman of Marriott International, for personally calling his peers in the industry and soliciting dollars to fund this travel industry recovery television ad *which had no government funding*.

In addition to the paid advertising, we organized a news media blitz that was incredibly successful. We put the ad onto a worldwide satellite feed and methodically pitched the story to the media, city by city, country by country. In each case we localized the Bush ad story by offering top travel industry executives for media interviews.

The goal of the news media campaign was two-fold: First, to get the ad to run for free as often as possible; and second, to call attention to the ad so that when it ran, viewers would notice and remember the message.

And notice and remember they did. A national survey showed that an incredible 70 percent of American consumers said they saw the Bush ad. And 55 percent of the adult population of the U.S. accurately described the message. That was an astounding success.

In addition to the ad campaign, we took the SeeAmerica message to three of the biggest international trade shows of the year: World Travel Market in the UK, JATA in Japan, and Braztoa in Brazil. And at each event, TIA hosted traditional U.S. "Thanksgiving" holiday events with the local media, tour operators and other key U.S. travel partners, thanking them for supporting travel to the U.S. during this time of crisis.

Week Ten: In week ten we announced a partnership between the industry and the U.S. Postal Service that leveraged the resources of both organizations to promote travel both within and to the United States.

The U.S. Postal Service agreed to print and release a set of stamps called Greetings from America featuring one stamp per each state for 50 unique stamps. TIA created a SeeAmerica Sweepstakes on the SeeAmerica.org web site. The Sweepstakes had 50 prizes of a one-week dream vacation for each of the 50 states, designed by each state tourism director. Each prize included a special dream itinerary with six nights hotel, a car rental and air transportation.

Posters showing the stamps and promoting the Sweepstakes were placed in state tourism information centers and in post offices around the country, guaranteeing exposure to more than 15 million people a day.

A PR campaign announcing the Greetings from America program generated more than 800 news stories with 70 million impressions. It ran in 209 U.S. television markets throughout the nation, including the top 25 markets.

In conclusion, what were the lessons we learned from this ten-week crisis communications campaign? They can be reduced to just four short points.

1. Develop a strategy and message and stay with it.

2. Engage the entire industry—and government too.

3. Leverage your resources so everyone can participate—in other words partner.

4. And finally, move quickly and take control of the situation— you can't afford to wait and let it control you.

Thank you.

Appendix C

Selected Travel and Tourism Print Media (with circulations over 43,000)

WEEKLY TRADE PERIODICALS

Aviation Week & Space Technology (103,313)

MONTHLY CONSUMER PERIODICALS

Bon Appetit (1.3 million)
Gourmet (975,216)
Travel & Leisure (965,977)
Food & Wine (943,710)
Conde Nast Traveler (779,061)
National Geographic Traveler (724,119) (8×/yr)

In-Flight Airline Magazines (many with average circulations of
    over 400,000 each)
Recreation News (106,122)

MONTHLY TRADE PERIODICALS

Cruising World (159,224)
Trains (130,385)
Restaurant Hospitality (117,719)
Successful Meetings (72,050)
Meetings & Conventions (M & C) (70,038)
Hotels (62,000)
Food Arts (58,000)
Business Traveler (55,000)
Recreation Management (50,000)

SEMIMONTHLY TRADE PERIODICAL

Hotel & Motel Management (53,386)

SEMIMONTHLY CONSUMER PERIODICAL

Wine Spectator (323,605)

BIMONTHLY CONSUMER PERIODICALS

AAA Going Places (3.8 million)
AAA World (2.2 million)
Departures (AMEX) (689,223)

Cruise Travel (153,645)
Elite Traveler (125,000)

Biweekly Consumer Periodical

Business Travel News (54,800)

Biweekly Trade Periodicals

Restaurant Business (129,000)
Lodging Hospitality (50,400) (13×/yr)
Travel Agent (46,300)
Travel Weekly (44,425)

(Source of circulations: *Bacon's 2005 Magazine Directory*)

Appendix D

Selected U.S. Universities Offering Hospitality and Tourism Education (and Their Concentrations)

Cornell University (Hotel Management)

Embry Riddle University (Aviation Mgt.)

George Washington University (Destination, Sport, and Meeting & Event Mgt.)

Michigan State University (Park, Recreation & Tourism)

New York University (Destination Mgt., Strategic Marketing)

Purdue University (Hotel and Tourism Mgt.)

Temple University (Tourism, Hospitality, Sport & Recreation)

University of Hawaii/Manoa (Travel & Tourism Mgt.)

University of Massachusetts (Hotel Mgt., Sports Mgt.)

University of Nevada/Las Vegas (Hotel Admin., Hospitality Ed., Convention & Meeting Planning, Casino Operations)

Virginia Tech (Hotel Mgt., Tourism Mgt.)

Appendix E

Selected Industry
Research/Statistical Sources

U.S. GOVERNMENT SOURCES

U.S. Department of Commerce
International Trade Administration
Office of Travel & Tourism Industries (OTTI)
14th and Constitution Ave., NW, Room 7025
Washington, D.C. 20230
202-482-0140
http:// tinet.ita.doc.gov

U.S. Department of the Interior
U.S. National Park Service
1849 C Street, NW
Washington, D.C. 20240
202-208-6843
www.nps.gov

PRIVATE SOURCES

J. D. Power & Associates
2625 Townsgate Rd.
Westlake Village, Calif. 91361
805-418-8000
www.jdpower.com

Smith Travel Research
735 East Main St.
Hendersonville, Tenn. 37035
615-824-8664
www.smithtravelresearch.com

Travel Industry Association of America (TIA)
1100 New York Ave., NW
Suite 450
Washington, D.C. 20005-3934
202-408-1255
www.tia.org

Travel and Tourism Research Association (TTRA)
P.O. Box 2133
Boise, Idaho 83701
208-429-9511
www.ttra.com

World Tourism Organization (WTO)
Capitan Haya 42
28020 Madrid, Spain
(34) 91-567-81-00
www.worldtourism.org/index.htm

Appendix F

Planning Press Trips That Pay Off

By Vivian A. Deuschl
Vice President of Public Relations
The Ritz-Carlton Hotel Co.
Chevy Chase, Md.

A traditional staple of PR practitioners, especially agencies, is the press trip. Properly planned and executed, press trips can still be one of the best ways of gaining important third-party endorsement from consumer and travel trade press. No matter how lavish or enjoyable a press trip is, if it does not result in significant media coverage, with quantifiable "return on investment" (ROI), it cannot be considered an effective PR tool for a destination, hotel, restaurant, attraction, or transportation mode. There *are* ways to ensure money spent on a press trip "pays off" with solid results. Here are some suggestions:

STARTING OUT

Planning for a press trip should begin at least three months ahead of time. PR professionals should ask themselves some basic questions before the process begins.

What audiences are you trying to influence? If you are looking to reach third parties (travel agents, tour operators, or meeting planners), your approach should be different than when trying to reach the end consumer.

What publications or other media do you need to invite? It is not a good idea to host press trips with a mix of consumer and trade media. Their interests are different, and a "one-size-fits-all" itinerary is usually not appealing to press who receive scores of invites every year.

Finding partners for a press trip is essential. Since costs can be very high to conduct an effective visit, teaming up with other tourism interests will make budgets stretch. It can also give journalists more of a reason to accept if multiple story angles are possible from a single trip. As an example: if a destination solicits tickets from an airline opening new routes to that region, this increases the newsworthiness of a press trip.

The financially-troubled legacy airlines are not as able to provide complimentary tickets as they once were. Also, they may question the effectiveness of press trips where coverage for them often is minimal. However, it is still possible for savvy PR practitioners to obtain tickets from airlines. A good example came in 2004 following a spate of tropical storms and hurricanes that battered Florida and the Caribbean. Several carriers serving those routes were willing to provide hotel partners, and destinations, with press trip tickets as a means of encouraging the press to see the region was not devastated, thus encouraging consumers to rebook once-canceled vacations.

Other important partnerships for a press trip can occur between hotels, convention and visitor bureaus/state tourism offices, attractions, and restaurants. While the official organizer or host of the trip sets the schedule, these partners can contribute complimentary or reduced meals and attractions that give the media a true indication of a destination's diversity. Having the opportunity to experience a "hot" new restaurant in a city is one of the features that makes a press trip invitation likely to be accepted by "A-list" media. Being offered a VIP preview tour of a city's major cultural attraction is another example of how partnerships make a press trip more appealing. Staying at a much talked about luxury hotel also is a plus. Travel journalists, as a whole, tend to be somewhat jaded. Their "been-there, done-that" attitude can make it a challenge—not an impossibility—to fill the trip with those who will produce results.

EXTENDING INVITATIONS

Deciding who to invite is a key component to planning a successful press trip. Since many media from publications including *Conde Nast Traveler* and *The New York Times* do not accept anything free, it is unlikely they will take a press trip. Such media usually travel on their own, at their publication's expense. While they may look to a hotel or destination for assistance with visitor information, or even a reduced rate, they prefer not to be part of a group.

However, some very excellent publications/broadcast outlets rely upon invitations that meet their expectations for a newsworthy experience. Ideally, press trip invitations should be extended to on-staff or freelance journalists with a confirmed assignment. It is totally acceptable to ask for a letter, on the publication's stationery, indicating the reporter has been assigned to do a story related to the press trip. On the other hand, experienced PR professionals may view a press trip invitation as an investment in the future, especially to freelancers. While they may not have an assignment at the time of the trip, the best freelancers can take one press trip and turn it into multiple stories. The landscape is littered with cautionary tales from PR executives who have been "burned" by writers who accepted the hospitality and never generated coverage. The better a PR person knows a reporter, the better are the chances the practitioner will know, in advance, if the journalist has a reliable track record.

Having said this, remember that coverage from a press trip may not always end up being positive. If the itinerary is so filled with "over the top" experiences, some journalists will feel they cannot write about their impressions because it will not be available to the average traveler.

When the reporters experience surly service, encounter tour escorts who are not familiar with a destination's feature, or an airline loses their luggage, PR people can expect most will "tell-it-like-it-is" to their readers. PR people must have realistic expectations for a press trip. This means letting their clients or supervisors know, ahead of time, that bad experiences can result in negative coverage or comments.

Most press trips are enjoyable experiences. Some can be less so, especially if one or more of the writers exhibits boorish behavior. This can happen when writers refuse to show up for scheduled events, insist on upgraded accommodations, or are unduly critical of their press trip hosts. While sending a journalist home early is a rare occurrence, it is an option if their behavior affects the dynamics of a press group visit. To avoid this type of situation, press trip hosts should make it clear—ahead of time and in writing—what is and is not included in the invitation. If two spa treatments are being offered, and the journalist insists on an additional massage or facial, the writer should expect to be asked to pay for them. On every press trip, a credit card imprint should be taken upon check in at the host hotel. This ensures personal, out-of-pocket expenses are not eventually absorbed by the hosts' budget.

Many journalists have their own complaints about press trips. The number one concern is lack of free time to pursue their own interests. They may want to go off on their own to research special story topics, or they may simply feel the need to avoid the "if it's Tuesday, it must be Belgium" reputation which comes with press trips that are overscheduled. Asking them what they would like to see and do, whether they have any health or dietary restrictions, and advising them of dress expectations are all advance steps that can help avoid problems.

ITINERARIES

Besides not overscheduling journalists, planning the itinerary has other important considerations.

Do not put them in a generic meeting room with a hotel general manager and make them watch a half-hour Power Point presentation. Instead, schedule a light lunch with the GM, where questions and answers can be shared in an impressive, yet informal atmosphere, like the hotel's outdoor garden. If promoting a destination, don't include stops at "tourist trap" attractions with long lines and big crowds. Introduce them to lesser known, but equally interesting, places in the city, escorted by a well-informed guide who can provide a unique commentary. If a journalist has requested specific interview opportunities, provide the time for them to have a one-on-one meeting that will help them with their story.

When filling these special requests, make sure every journalist has similar opportunities, so there is no chance of others feeling slighted. No matter which publication they represent, journalists on a press trip should be made to feel valued and appreciated. They should never return from a trip to write their story believing there was a "pecking order of perks" on the part of the PR person. This is especially true on a trip where on-staff writers and freelancers are included. Some freelancers resent being treated like second-class citizens, and that is a post-press trip feeling they should never have.

POST-TRIP FOLLOW-UP

Once the journalists have returned home, a follow-up note or phone call from the PR person is both polite and politic. Writers will usually be honest about their experience, sharing insights that can be useful for future trips. Asking them to send proof sheets, or alerting you to when the coverage comes out, can be viewed by some as annoying, but often that is the only way for the PR person to know if their carefully planned press trip really did "pay off."

Index